Edmund Spenser

Epithalamion

Edited by
Robert Beum
St. Dunstan's University

The Merrill Literary
Casebook Series
Edward P. J. Corbett, Editor

Charles E. Merrill Publishing Company
Columbus, Ohio
A Bell & Howell Company

Copyright © 1968 by CHARLES E. MERRILL PUBLISHING COMPANY, Columbus, Ohio. All rights reserved. No part of this book may be reproduced in any form or by any process without permission in writing from the publisher.

Standard Book Number: 675-09561-1
Library of Congress Catalog Number: 68-56013

1 2 3 4 5 6 7 8 9 10 — 72 71 70 69 68

Printed in the United States of America

Foreword

The Charles E. Merrill Literary Casebook Series deals with short literary works, arbitrarily defined here as "works which can be easily read in a single sitting." Accordingly, the series will concentrate on poems, short stories, brief dramas, and literary essays. These casebooks are designed to be used in literature courses or in practical criticism courses where the instructor wants to expose his students to an extensive and intensive study of a single, short work or in composition courses where the instructor wants to expose his students to the discipline of writing a research paper on a literary text.

All of the casebooks in the series follow this format: (1) foreword; (2) general instructions for the writing of a research paper; (3) the editor's Introduction; (4) the text of the literary work; (5) a number of critical articles on the literary work; (6) suggested topics for short papers on the literary work; (7) suggested topics for long (10-15 pages) papers on the literary work; (8) a selective bibliography of additional readings on the literary work. Some of the casebooks, especially those dealing with poetry, may carry an additional section, which contains such features as variant versions of the work, a closely related literary work, comments by the author and his contemporaries on the work.

So that students might simulate first-hand research in library copies of books and bound periodicals, each of the critical articles carries full bibliographical information at the bottom of the first page of the article, and the text of the article carries the actual page-numbers of the original source. A notation like /131/ after a word in the text indicates that *after* that word in the original source the article went over to page 131. All of the text between that number and the next number, /132/, can be taken as occurring on page 131 of the original source.

Edward P.J. Corbett
General Editor

General Instructions For A Research Paper

If your instructor gives you any specific directions about the format of your research paper that differ from the directions given here, you are, of course, to follow his directions. Otherwise, you can observe these directions with the confidence that they represent fairly standard conventions.

A research paper represents a student's synthesis of his reading in a number of primary and secondary works, with an indication, in footnotes, of the source of quotations used in the paper or of facts cited in paraphrased material. A *primary* source is the text of a work as it issued from the pen of the author or some document contemporary with the work. The following, for instance, would be considered primary sources: a manuscript copy of the work; first editions of the work and any subsequent editions authorized by the writer; a modern scholarly edition of the text; an author's comment about his work in letters, memoirs, diaries, journals, or periodicals; published comments on the work by the author's contemporaries. A *secondary* source would be any interpretation, explication, or evaluation of the work printed, usually several years after the author's death, in critical articles and books, in literary histories, and in biographies of the author. In this casebook, the text of the work, any variant versions of it, any commentary on the work by the author himself or his contemporaries may be considered as primary sources; the editor's Introduction, the articles from journals, and the excerpts from books are to be considered secondary sources. The paper that you eventually write will become a secondary source.

Plagiarism

The cardinal sin in the academic community is plagiarism. The rankest form of plagiarism is the verbatim reproduction of someone else's words without any indication that the passage is a quotation. A lesser but still serious form of plagiarism is to report, in your own words, the fruits of someone else's research without acknowledging the source of your information or interpretation.

You can take this as an inflexible rule: every verbatim quotation in your paper must be either enclosed in quotation marks or single-spaced and inset from the left-hand margin and must be followed by a footnote number. Students who merely change a few words or phrases in a quotation and present the passage as their own work are still guilty of plagiarism. Passages of genuine paraphrase must be footnoted too if the information or idea or interpretation contained in the paraphrase cannot be presumed to be known by ordinary educated people or at least by readers who would be interested in the subject you are writing about.

The penalties for plagiarism are usually very severe. Don't run the risk of a failing grade on the paper or even of a failing grade in the course.

Lead-Ins

Provide a lead-in for all quotations. Failure to do so results in a serious breakdown in coherence. The lead-in should at least name the person who is being quoted. The ideal lead-in, however, is one that not only names the person but indicates the pertinence of the quotation.

Examples:

    (typical lead-in for a single-spaced, inset quotation)

    Irving Babbitt makes this observation about Flaubert's attitude toward women:

(typical lead-in for quotation worked into the frame of one's sentence)

    Thus the poet sets out to show how the present age, as George Anderson puts it, "negates the values of the earlier revolution."[7]

Full Names

The first time you mention anyone in a paper give the full name of the person. Subsequently you may refer to him by his last name.

Examples: First allusion—Ronald S. Crane
            Subsequent allusions—Professor Crane, as Crane says.

Ellipses

Lacunae in a direct quotation are indicated with *three spaced periods*, in addition to whatever punctuation mark was in the text at the point where you truncated the quotation. *Hit the space-bar of your typewriter between each period.* Usually there is no need to put the ellipsis-periods at the beginning or the end of a quotation.

Example: "The poets were not striving to communicate with their audience; . . . By and large, the Romantics were seeking . . . to express their unique personalities."[8]

Brackets

Brackets are used to enclose any material interpolated into a direct quotation. The abbreviation *sic*, enclosed in brackets, indicates that the error of spelling, grammar, or fact in a direct quotation has been copied as it was in the source being quoted. If your typewriter does not have special keys for brackets, draw the brackets neatly with a pen.

Examples: "He [Theodore Baum] maintained that Confucianism [the primary element in Chinese philosophy] aimed at teaching each individual to accept his lot in life."[12]

"Paul Revear [sic] made his historic ride on April 18, 1875 [sic]."[15]

Summary Footnote

A footnote number at the end of a sentence which is not enclosed in quotation marks indicates that only *that* sentence is being documented in the footnote. If you want to indicate that the footnote documents more than one sentence, put a footnote number at the end of the *first* sentence of the paraphrased passage and use some formula like this in the footnote:

[16] For the information presented in this and the following paragraph, I am indebted to Marvin Magalaner, <u>Time of Apprenticeship: the Fiction of Young James Joyce</u> (London, 1959), pp. 81-93.

Citing the Edition

The edition of the author's work being used in a paper should always be cited in the first footnote that documents a quotation from that work. You can obviate the need for subsequent footnotes to that edition by using some formula like this:

⁴ Nathaniel Hawthorne, "Young Goodman Brown," as printed in <u>Young Goodman Brown</u>, ed. Thomas E. Connolly, Charles E. Merrill Literary Casebooks (Columbus, Ohio, 1968), pp. 3-15. This edition will be used throughout the paper, and hereafter all quotations from this book will be documented with a page-number in parentheses at the end of the quotation.

Notetaking

Although all the material you use in your paper may be contained in this casebook, you will find it easier to organize your paper if you work from notes written on 3 x 5 or 4 x 6 cards. Besides, you should get practice in the kind of notetaking you will have to do for other termpapers, when you will have to work from books and articles in, or on loan from, the library.

An ideal note is a self-contained note—one which has all the information you would need if you used anything from that note in your paper. A note will be self-contained if it carries the following information:

(1) The information or quotation *accurately* copied.
(2) Some system for distinguishing direct quotation from paraphrase.
(3) All the bibliographical information necessary for documenting that note—full name of the author, title, volume number (if any), place of publication, publisher, publication date, page numbers.
(4) If a question covered more than one page in the source, the note-card should indicate which part of the quotation occurred on one page and which part occurred on the next page. The easiest way to do this is to put the next page number in parentheses after the last word on one page and before the first word on the next page.

In short, your note should be so complete that you would never have to go back to the original source to gather any piece of information about that note.

Footnote Forms

The footnote forms used here follow the conventions set forth in the *MLA Style Sheet*, Revised Edition, ed. William Riley Parker, which is now used by more than 100 journals and more than thirty university presses in the United States. Copies of this pamphlet can be purchased for fifty cents from your university bookstore or from the Modern Language Association, 62 Fifth Avenue, New York, N.Y. 10011. If your teacher or your institution prescribes a modified form of this footnoting system, you should, of course, follow that system.

A primary footnote, the form used the first time a source is cited, supplies four pieces of information: (1) author's name, (2) title of the source, (3) publication information, (4) specific location in the source of the information or quotation. A secondary footnote is the shorthand form of documentation after the source has been cited in full the first time.

Your instructor may permit you to put all your footnotes on separate pages at the end of your paper. But he may want to give you practice in putting footnotes at the bottom of the page. Whether the footnotes are put at the end of the paper or at the bottom of the page, they should observe this format of spacing: (1) the first line of each footnote should be indented, usually the same number of spaces as your paragraph indentations; (2) all subsequent lines of the footnote should start at the lefthand margin; (3) there should be single-spacing within each footnote and double-spacing between each footnote.

Example:

[10] Ruth Wallerstein, <u>Richard Crashaw: A Study in Style and Poetic Development</u>, University of Wisconsin Studies in Language and Literature, No. 37 (Madison, 1935), p. 52.

Primary Footnotes

(The form to be used the *first* time a work is cited)

[1] Paull F. Baum, <u>Ten Studies in the Poetry of Matthew Arnold</u> (Durham, N.C., 1958), p. 37.

(book by a single author; p. is the abbreviation of *page*)

[2] René Wellek and Austin Warren, <u>Theory of Literature</u> (New York, 1949), pp. 106-7.

(book by two authors; pp. is the abbreviation of *pages*)

³ William Hickling Prescott, <u>History of the Reign of Philip the Second, King of Spain,</u> ed. John Foster Kirk (Philadelphia, 1871), II, 47.

(an edited work of more than one volume; *ed.* is the abbreviation for "edited by"; note that whenever a volume number is cited, the abbreviation p. or pp. is *not* used in front of the page number)

⁴ John Pick, ed., <u>The Windhover</u> (Columbus, Ohio 1968), p. 4.

(form for quotation from an editor's Introduction—as, for instance, in this casebook series; here *ed.* is the abbreviation for "editor")

⁵ A.S.P. Woodhouse, "Nature and Grace in <u>The Faerie Queen,</u>" in <u>Elizabethan Poetry: Modern Essays in Criticism</u>, ed. Paul J. Alpers (New York, 1967), pp. 346-7.

(chapter or article from an edited collection)

⁶ Morton D. Paley, "Tyger of Wrath," <u>PMLA</u>, LXXXI (December, 1966), 544.

(an article from a periodical; note that because the volume number is cited no p. or pp. precedes the page number; the titles of periodicals are often abbreviated in footnotes but are spelled out in the Bibliography; here, for instance, *PMLA* is the abbreviation for *Publications of the Modern Language Association*)

Secondary Footnotes

(Abbreviated footnote forms to be used after a work has been cited once in full)

⁷ Baum, p. 45.

(abbreviated form for work cited in footnote #1; note that the secondary footnote is indented the same number of spaces as the first line of primary footnotes)

⁸ Wellek and Warren, pp. 239-40.

(abbreviated form for work cited in footnote #2)

⁹ Prescott, II, 239.

(abbreviated form for work cited in footnote #3; because this is a multi-volume work, the volume number must be given in addition to the page number)

¹⁰ <u>Ibid.</u>, p. 245.

(refers to the immediately preceding footnote—that is, to page 245 in the second volume of Prescott's history; *ibid.* is the abbreviation of the Latin adverb *ibidem* meaning "in the same place"; note that this abbreviation is italicized or underlined and that it is followed by a period, because it is an abbreviation)

[11] <u>Ibid</u>., III, 103.
(refers to the immediately preceding footnote—that is, to Prescott's work again; there must be added to *ibid.* only what changes from the preceding footnote; here the volume and page changed: note that there is no p. before 103, because a volume number was cited)

[12] Baum, pp. 47-50.
(refers to the same work cited in footnote #7 and ultimately to the work cited in full in footnote #1)

[13] Paley, p. 547.
(refers to the article cited in footnote #6)

[14] Rebecca P. Parkin, "Mythopoeic Activity in the <u>Rape of the Lock</u>," <u>ELH</u>, XXI (March, 1954), 32.
(since this article from the *Journal of English Literary History* has not been previously cited in full, it must be given in full here)

[15] <u>Ibid</u>., pp. 33-4.
(refers to Parkin's article in the immediately preceding footnote)

Bibliography Forms

Note carefully the differences in bibliography forms from footnote forms: (1) the last name of the author is given first, since bibliography items are arranged alphabetically according to the surname of the author (in the case of two or more authors of a work, only the name of the first author is reversed); (2) the first line of each bibliography item starts at the lefthand margin; subsequent lines are indented; (3) periods are used instead of commas, and parentheses do not enclose publication information; (4) the publisher is given in addition to the place of publication; (5) the first and last pages of articles and chapters are given; (6) most of the abbreviations used in footnotes are avoided in the Bibliography.

The items are arranged here alphabetically as they would appear in the Bibliography of your paper.

Baum, Paull F. <u>Ten Studies in the Poetry of Matthew Arnold</u>. Durham, N.C.: University of North Carolina Press, 1958.

Paley, Morton D. "Tyger of Wrath," *Publications of the Modern Language Association*, LXXXI (December, 1966), 540-51.

Parkin, Rebecca P. "Mythopoeic Activity in the *Rape of the Lock*," *Journal of English Literary History*, XXI (March, 1954), 30-8.

Pick, John, editor. *The Windhover*. Columbus, Ohio: Charles E. Merrill Publishing Company, 1968.

Prescott, William Hickling. *History of the Reign of Philip the Second, King of Spain*. Edited by John Foster Kirk. 3 volumes. Philadelphia: J.B. Lippincott and Company, 1871.

Wellek, René and Austin Warren. *Theory of Literature*. New York: Harcourt, Brace & World, Inc., 1949.

Woodhouse, A.S.P. "Nature and Grace in *The Faerie Queene*," in *Elizabethan Poetry: Modern Essays in Criticism*. Edited by Paul J. Alpers. New York: Oxford University Press, 1967, pp. 345-79.

If the form for some work that you are using in your paper is not given in these samples of footnote and bibliography entries, ask your instructor for advice as to the proper form.

Contents

Introduction	1
Epithalamion **by Edmund Spenser**	3
Notes	16
General	
Robert Kellogg and Oliver Steele, *Epithalamion: Introduction*, 1965	25
C. S. Lewis, From *English Literature in the Sixteenth Century, Excluding Drama*, 1954	29
Émile Legouis, From *Spenser*, 1926	31
J. W. Mackail, From *The Springs of Helicon*, 1909	32
Cortlandt Van Winkle, From *Epithalamion (Introduction)*, 1926	33
Origins, Genre	
Thomas M. Greene, *Spenser and the Epithalamic Convention*	37
George Puttenham, *The Maner of Reioysings at Mariages and Weddings*	53
Philosophy	
E. E. Stoll, From *Poets & Playwrights: Shakespeare, Jonson, Spenser, Milton*, 1930	59
Virgil K. Whitaker, From *The Religious Basis of Spenser's Thought*, 1950	69
W. L. Renwick, From *Daphnäida and Other Poems*, 1929	72
John Smith Harrison, From *Platonism in English Poetry of the Sixteenth and Seventeenth Centuries*, 1915	77
Imagery and Symbolism	
Israel Baroway, *The Imagery of Spenser and the Song of Songs*, 1934	81

Language, Style

C. S. Lewis, From *English Literature in the Sixteenth Century, Excluding Drama*, 1954 — **107**

Herbert David Rix, From *Rhetoric in Spenser's Poetry*, 1940 — **109**

Hallett Smith, *The Use of Conventions in Spenser's Minor Poems*, 1961 — **111**

Versification

Robert Beum, *Some Observations on Spenser's Verse Forms*, 1963 — **123**

John Erskine, From *The Elizabethan Lyric*, 1905 — **130**

Suggestions for Papers — **132**

Additional Readings — **135**

Appendices: I, II — **139**

Introduction

Few pieces of literature have been so highly and so consistently praised as the *Epithalamion*, a poem Edmund Spenser wrote as a wedding gift for his bride nearly four centuries ago. Until recently, there was no question but that the poet's poet had achieved his difficult aim: here, if anywhere, was an "endless monument." "The most gorgeous jewel in the treasure-house of the Renaissance," Émile Legouis, a scholar not usually inclined toward dithyrambic praise, calls it; "the most beautiful of all his poems," says W. B. Yeats in one of his own most beautiful and wisest essays. The *Epithalamion* is widely available: practically every anthology of English poetry and every "survey" textbook carries it. Teachers have taught it and students have read it.

And yet one receives the distinct impression that during the past few decades the poem has not been read well or taught well, that it has not "taken" as other Renaissance poems—say, Donne's "Canonization" or Marvell's "To His Coy Mistress"—have. The teacher seldom gives to Spenser as much time as he gives to Donne; and rare, apparently, is the graduate student who is excited by the *Epithalamion*.

Undoubtedly there are many reasons for this neglect or coolness. To suggest only a few: ignorance and unpreparedness—it is now possible to obtain an advanced degree in English literature and at the same time to avoid or very nearly avoid Spenser (or at least any of Spenser except Book I of the *Faerie Queene*); ultra-modernmindedness—Spenser, a poet of slow movement, opulence, and little irony, is not for the reader who has given his whole heart to the speed and smartness of secular-egalitarian technocracies; hyperintellectualism—Spenser's unambiguous and rather traditional language provides the brilliant critical exegete with few opportunities to perform his bravura. The really important point, however, is that the present tendency to give only a passing attention to Spenser's ode seems to derive in part from the conviction (or intimation) that the poem is not, in fact, the eminently worthy piece that tradition has reported it to be. Though few clear or mapor charges have been explicitly drawn up, the poem has become somewhat controversial.

If the *Epithalamion* is as good a poem as tradition tells us it is, then we ought to be reading it; if there has now arisen intelligent disagreement about the poem's value, then to make the argument articulate and to decide who has the better of it, again we ought to be reading the poem.

And we might, at the same time, fortify ourselves by reading some of the things that have already been well said about the *Epithalamion*. The present book offers a selection from what the editor deems to be the most cogent and interesting commentary (in English) that has been made on the poem. Hopefully, the essays and excerpts collected here are sufficiently varied to enable the reader to approach the poem more wisely, no matter what aspect of the ode fascinates or troubles him.

Certainly part of the difficulty the poem has run into is the mere dearth of readily available scholarly and critical materials on Spenser's minor poems. It is the enhancement of *understanding* to which the present anthology primarily devotes itself. The book has no desire to try to create an ephemeral and somewhat sensationalist interest by exaggerating the controversy (or perhaps only rumor of controversy) that has developed around the *Epithalamion*. At the same time, the editor would be less than honest (and less than happy) to claim for himself a grey and neutral status: the book is also presented in the faith that Spenser's bridal present, for which he apologized, needs in fact no apologies, and will again be widely recognized as one of the most challenging and rewarding poems anyone can take up from the whole millennium of English literature. The *Epithalamion* does, after all, open up many possibilities. It can teach *Spenser,* for it is completely typical of his matter and manner, and is also Spenser at his best. It can ask us to consider the possibility that the ironic, hyper-succinct, obscure, novelty-seeking Renaissance Metaphysicals may not have located the only good ore in the mine. It can show us in microcosm the essential character of the European Renaissance. It can demonstrate the appeal generated by *balance,* the appeal of strong personal emotion avoiding the pitfalls of sentimentality, idiosyncrasy, and obscurity by means of the steadying influence of depersonalizing conventions. It can teach the *ode* as a verse genre, or illustrate a technical mastery of the art of prosody. It can waken the student to the complex possibilites of human love.

Epithalamion

1

Ye learned sisters which haue oftentimes
beene to me ayding, others to adorne:
Whom ye thought worthy of your gracefull rymes,
That euen the greatest did not greatly scorne
To heare theyr names sung in your simple layes,
But ioyed in theyr prayse.
And when ye list your owne mishaps to mourne,
Which death, or loue, or fortunes wreck did rayse,
Your string could soone to sadder tenor turne,
And teach the woods and waters to lament   10
Your dolefull dreriment.
Now lay those sorrowfull complaints aside,
And hauing all your heads with girland crownd,
Helpe me mine owne loues prayses to resound,
Ne let the same of any be enuide,
So Orpheus did for his owne bride,
So I vnto my selfe alone will sing,
The woods shall to me answer and my Eccho
   ring.

2

Early before the worlds light giuing lampe,
His golden beame vpon the hils doth spred,   20
Hauing disperst the nights vnchearefull dampe,
Doe ye awake and with fresh lusty hed,
Go to the bowre of my beloued loue,
My truest turtle doue,
Bid her awake; for Hymen is awake,
And long since ready forth his maske to moue,
With his bright Tead that flames with many a
   flake,

And many a bachelor to waite on him,
In theyr fresh garments trim.
Bid her awake therefore and soone her dight, 30
For lo the wished day is come at last,
That shall for al the paynes and sorrowes past,
Pay to her vsury of long delight,
And whylest she doth her dight,
Doe ye to her of ioy and solace sing,
That all the woods may answer and your eccho
   ring.

3

Bring with you all the Nymphes that you can
   heare
both of the riuers and the forrests greene:
And of the sea that neighbours to her neare,
Al with gay girlands goodly wel beseene. 40
And let them also with them bring in hand,
Another gay girland
For my fayre loue of lillyes and of roses,
Bound trueloue wize with a blew silke riband.
And let them make great store of bridale poses,
And let them eeke bring store of other flowers
To deck the bridale bowers.
And let the ground whereas her foot shall tread,
For feare the stones her tender foot should wrong
Be strewed with fragrant flowers all along, 50
And diapred lyke the discolored mead.
Which done, doe at her chamber dore awayt,
For she will waken strayt,
The whiles doe ye this song vnto her sing,
The woods shall to you answer and your Eccho
   ring.

4

Ye Nymphes of Mulla which with carefull heed,
The siluer scaly trouts doe tend full well,
and greedy pikes which vse therein to feed,
(Those trouts and pikes all others doo excell)
And ye likewise which keepe the rushy lake, 60
Where none doo fishes take,
Bynd vp the locks the which hang scatterd light,

And in his waters which your mirror make,
Behold your faces as the christall bright,
That when you come whereas my loue doth lie,
No blemish she may spie.
And eke ye lightfoot mayds which keepe the dere,
That on the hoary mountayne vse to towre,
And the wylde wolues which seeke them to deuoure,
With your steele darts doo chace fró comming
   neer 70
Be also present heere,
To helpe to decke her and to help to sing,
That all the woods may answer and your eccho
   ring.

5

Wake now my loue, awake; for it is time,
The Rosy Morne long since left Tithones bed,
All ready to her siluer coche to clyme,
And Phoebus gins to shew his glorious hed.
Hark how the cheerefull birds do chaunt theyr
   laies
And carroll of loues praise.
The merry Larke hir mattins sings aloft, 80
The thrush replyes, the Mauis descant playes,
The Ouzell shrills, the Ruddock warbles soft,
So goodly all agree with sweet consent,
To this dayes merriment.
Ah my deere loue why doe ye sleepe thus long,
When meeter were that ye should now awake,
T'awayt the comming of your ioyous make,
And hearken to the birds louelearned song,
The deawy leaues among.
For they of ioy and pleasance to you sing, 90
That all the woods them answer & theyr eccho
   ring.

6

My loue is now awake out of her dreame,
and her fayre eyes like stars that dimmed were
With darksome cloud, now shew theyr goodly
   beames
More bright then Hesperus his head doth rere.

Come now ye damzels, daughters of delight,
Helpe quickly her to dight,
But first come ye fayre houres which were begot
In Ioues sweet paradice, of Day and Night,
Which doe the seasons of the yeare allot, 100
And al that euer in this world is fayre
Doe make and still repayre.
And ye three handmayds of the Cyprian Queene,
The which doe still adorne her beauties pride,
Helpe to addorne my beautifullest bride
And as ye her array, still throw betweene
Some graces to be seene,
And as ye vse to Venus, to her sing,
The whiles the woods shal answer & your eccho
   ring.

7

Now is my loue all ready forth to come, 110
Let all the virgins therefore well awayt,
And ye fresh boyes that tend vpon her groome
Prepare your selues; for he is comming strayt.
Set all your things in seemely good aray
Fit for so ioyfull day,
The ioyfulst day that euer sunne did see.
Faire Sun, shew forth thy fauourable ray,
And let thy lifull heat not feruent be
For feare of burning her sunshyny face,
Her beauty to disgrace. 120
O fayrest Phoebus, father of the Muse,
If euer I did honour thee aright,
Or sing the thing, that mote thy mind delight,
Doe not thy seruants simple boone refuse,
But let this day let this one day be myne,
Let all the rest be thine.
Then I thy souerayne prayses loud wil sing,
That all the woods shal answer and theyr eccho
   ring.

8

Harke how the Minstrels gin to shril aloud,
Their merry Musick that resounds from far, 130

The pipe, the tabor, and the trembling Croud,
That well agree withouten breach or iar.
But most of all the Damzels doe delite,
When they their tymbrels smyte,
And thereunto doe daunce and carrol sweet,
That all the sences they doe rauish quite,
The whyles the boyes run vp and downe the street,
Crying aloud with strong confused noyce,
As if it were one voyce.
Hymen io Hymen, Hymen they do shout,   140
That euen to the heauens theyr shouting shrill
Doth reach, and all the firmament doth fill,
To which the people standing all about,
As in approuance doe thereto applaud
And loud aduaunce her laud,
And euermore they Hymen Hymen sing,
    that al the woods them answer and theyr eccho ring.

9

Loe where she comes along with portly pace,
Lyke Phoebe from her chamber of the East,
Arysing forth to run her mighty race,   150
Clad all in white, that seems a virgin best.
So well it her beseemes that ye would weene
Some angell she had beene.
Her long loose yellow locks lyke golden wyre,
Sprinckled with perle, and perling flowres a
    tweene,
Doe lyke a golden mantle her attyre,
And being crowned with girland greene,
Seem lyke some mayden Queene,
Her modest eyes abashed to behold
So many gazers, as on her do stare,   160
Vpon the lowly ground affixed are.
Ne dare lift vp her countenance too bold,
But blush to heare her prayses sung so loud,
So farre from being proud.
Nathlesse doe ye still loud her prayses sing,
    That all the woods may answer and your eccho ring.

10

Tell me ye merchants daughters did ye see
So fayre a creature in your towne before,
So sweet, so louely, and so mild as she,
Adornd with beautyes grace and vertues store, 170
Her goodly eyes lyke Saphryes shining bright,
Her forehead yuory white,
Her cheekes lyke apples which the sun hath rudded,
Her lips lyke cherryes charming men to byte,
Her brest like to a bowle of creame vncrudded,
Her paps like lyllies budded,
Her snowie necke lyke to a marble toure,
And all her body like a pallace fayre,
Ascending vppe with many a stately stayre,
To honors seat and chastities sweet bowre. 180
Why stand ye still ye virgins in amaze,
Vpon her so to gaze,
Whiles ye forget your former lay to sing,
To which the woods did answer and your eccho ring.

11

Bvt if ye saw that which no eyes can see,
The inward beauty of her liuely spright,
Garnisht with heauenly guifts of high degree,
Much more then would ye wonder at that sight,
And stand astonisht like to those which red
Medusaes mazeful hed. 190
There dwels sweet loue and constant chastity,
Vnspotted fayth and comely womanhood,
Regard of honour and mild modesty,
There vertue raynes as Queene in royal throne,
And giueth lawes alone.
The which the base affections doe obay,
And yeeld theyr seruices vnto her will,
Ne thought of thing vncomely euer may
Thereto approch to tempt her mind to ill.
Had ye once seene these her celestial threasures, 200
And vnreuealed pleasures,
Then would ye wonder and her prayses sing,

That al the woods should answer and your echo
   ring.

12

Open the temple gates vnto my loue,
Open them wide that she may enter in,
And all the postes adorne as doth behoue,
And all the pillours deck with girlands trim,
For to recyue this Saynt with honour dew,
That commeth in to you,
With trembling steps and humble reuerence,   210
She commeth in, before th' almighties vew,
Of her ye virgins learne obedience,
When so ye come into those holy places,
To humble your proud faces
Bring her vp to th' high altar that she may,
The sacred ceremonies there partake,
The which do endlesse matrimony make,
And let the roring Organs loudly play;
The praises of the Lord in liuely notes,
The whiles with hollow throates.   220
The Choristers the ioyous Antheme sing,
That al the woods may answere and their eccho
   ring

13

Behold whiles she before the altar stands
Hearing the holy priest that to her speakes
And blesseth her with his two happy hands,
How the red roses flush vp in her cheekes,
And the pure snow with goodly vermill stayne,
Like crimsin dyde in grayne,
That euen th'Angels which continually,
About the sacred Altare doe remaine,   230
Forget their seruice and about her fly,
Ofte peeping in her face that seemes more fayre,
The more they on it stare.
But her sad eyes still fastened on the ground,
Are gouerned with goodly modesty,
That suffers not one looke to glaunce awry,
Which may let in a little thought vnsownd,

Why blush ye loue to giue to me your hand,
The pledge of all our band,
Sing ye sweet Angels Alleluya sing, 240
That all the woods may answere and your eccho
   ring.

14

Now al is done; bring home the bride againe
bring home the triumph of our victory,
Bring home with you the glory of her gaine,
With ioyance bring her and with iollity.
Neuer had man more ioyfull day then this,
Whom heauen would heape with blis.
Make feast therefore now all this liue long day,
This day for euer to me holy is,
Poure out the wine without restraint or stay, 250
Poure not by cups, but by the belly full,
Poure out to all that wull,
And sprinckle all the postes and wals with wine,
That they may sweat, and drunken be withall.
Crowne ye God Bacchus with a coronall,
And Hymen also crowne with wreathes of vine,
And let the Graces daunce vnto the rest;
For they can doo it best:
The whiles the maydens doe theyr carroll sing,
To which the woods shal answer & theyr eccho
   ring. 260

15

Ring ye the bels, ye yong men of the towne,
And leaue your wonted labors for this day:
This day is holy; doe ye write it dovvne,
that ye for euer it remember may.
This day the sunne is in his chiefest hight,
With Barnaby the bright,
From whence declining daily by degrees,
He somewhat loseth of his heat and light,
When once the Crab behind his back he sees.
But for this time it ill ordained was, 270
To chose the longest day in all the yeare,
And shortest night, when longest fitter weare:

Epithalamion

Yet neuer day so long, but late would passe.
Ring ye the bels, to make it weare away,
And bonefiers make all day,
And daunce about them, and about them sing:
  that all the woods may answer, and your eccho
    ring.

16

Ah when will this long vveary day haue end,
and lende me leaue to come vnto my loue?
Hovv slovvly do the houres theyr numbers
  spend?   280
How slowly does sad Time his feathers moue?
Hast thee O fayrest Planet to thy home
Within the Western fome:
Thy tyred steedes long since haue need of rest.
Long though it be, at last I see it gloome,
And the bright euening star with golden creast
Appeare out of the East.
Fayre childe of beauty, glorious lampe of loue
That all the host of heauen in rankes doost lead,
And guydest louers through the nightes dread,   290
How chearefully thou lookest from aboue,
And guydest louers through the nightes dread,
As ioying in the sight
Of these glad many which for ioy doe sing,
  That all the woods them answer and their echo
    ring.

17

Now ceasse ye damsels your delights forepast;
Enough is it, that all the day was youres:
Now day is doen, and night is nighing fast:
Now bring the Bryde into the brydall boures.
Now night is come, now soone her disaray,   300
And in her bed her lay;
Lay her in lillies and in violets,
And silken courteins ouer her display,
And odourd sheetes, and Arras couerlets,
Behold how goodly my faire loue does ly

In proud humility;
Like vnto Maia, when as Ioue her tooke,
In Tempe, lying on the flowry gras,
Twixt sleepe and wake, after she weary was,
With bathing in the Acidalian brooke.   310
Now it is night, ye damsels may be gon,
And leaue my loue alone,
And leaue likewise your former lay to sing:
The woods no more shal answere, nor your echo
  ring

18

Now welcome night, thou night so long ex-
  pected,
that long daies labour doest at last defray,
And all my cares, which cruell loue collected,
Hast sumd in one, and cancelled for aye:
Spread thy broad wing ouer my loue and me,
that no man may vs see,   320
And in thy sable mantle vs enwrap,
From feare of perill and foule horror free.
Let no false treason seeke vs to entrap,
Nor any dread disquiet once annoy
the safety of our ioy:
But let the night be calme and quietsome,
Without tempestuous storms or sad afray:
Lyke as when Ioue with fayre Alcmena lay,
When he begot the great Tirynthian groome:
Or lyke as when he with thy selfe did lie,   330
And begot Maiesty.
And let the mayds and yongmen cease to sing:
Ne let the woods them answer, nor theyr eccho
  ring.

19

Let no lamenting cryes, nor dolefull teares,
Be heard all night within nor yet without:
Ne let false whispers breeding hidden feares,
Breake gentle sleepe with misconcieued dout.
Let no deluding dreames, nor dreadful sights

Make sudden sad affrights;
Ne let housefyres, nor lightnings helpelesse
    harmes, 340
Ne let the Ponke, nor other euill sprights,
Ne let mischiuous witches with theyr charmes,
Ne let hob Goblins, names whose sence we see not,
Fray vs with things that be not.
Let not the shriech Oule, nor the Storke be
    heard:
Nor the night Rauen that still deadly yels,
Nor damned ghosts cald vp with mighty spels,
Nor griesly vultures make vs once affeard:
Ne let th' unpleasant Quyre of Frogs still croking
Make vs to wish theyr choking. 350
Let none of these theyr drery accents sing;
Ne let the woods them answer, nor theyr eccho
    ring.

20

But let stil Silence trew night watches keepe,
That sacred peace may in assurance rayne,
And tymely sleep, when it is tyme to sleepe,
May poure his limbs forth on the pleasant playne,
The whiles an hundred little winged loues,
Like diuers fethered doues,
Shall fly and flutter round about the bed,
And in the secret darke, that none reproues, 360
Their prety stealthes shal worke, & snares shal
    spread
To filch away sweet snatches of delight,
Conceald through couert night.
Ye sonnes of Venus, play your sports at will,
For greedy pleasure, careless of your toyes,
Thinks more upon her paradise of ioyes,
Then what ye do, albe it good or ill.
All night therefore attend your merry play,
For it will soone be day:
Now none doth hinder you, that say or sing, 370
Ne will the woods now answer, nor your Eccho
    ring.

21

Who is the same, which at my window peepes?
Or whose is that faire face, that shines so bright,
Is it not Cinthia, she that neuer sleepes,
But walkes about high heauen al the night?
O fayrest goddesse, do thou not enuy
My loue with me to spy:
For thou likewise didst loue, though now vnthought,
And for a fleece of woll, which priuily,
The Latmian shephard once vnto thee brought,   380
His pleasures with thee wrought.
Therefore to vs be fauorable now;
And sith of wemens labours thou hast charge,
And generation goodly dost enlarge,
Encline they will t'effect our wishfull vow,
And the chast wombe informe with timely seed,
That may our comfort breed:
Till which we cease our hopefull hap to sing,
Ne let the woods vs answere, nor our Eccho ring,

22

And thou great Iuno, which with awful might   390
the lawes of wedlock still dost patronize,
And the religion of the faith first plight
With sacred rites hast taught to solemnize:
and eeke for comfort often called art
Of women in their smart,
Eternally bind thou this louely band,
And all thy blessings vnto vs impart.
And thou glad Genius, in whose gentle hand,
The bridale bowre and geniall bed remaine,
Without blemish or staine,   400
And the sweet pleasures of theyr loues delight
With secret ayde doest succour and supply,
Till they bring forth the fruitfull progeny,
Send vs the timely fruit of this same night.
And thou fayre Hebe, and thou Hymen free,
Grant that it may so be.
Til which we cease your further prayse to sing,
Ne any woods shal answer, nor your Eccho ring,

23

And ye high heauens, the temple of the gods,
In which a thousand torches flaming bright 410
Doe burne, that to vs wretched earthly clods:
In dreadful darknesse lend desired light;
And all ye powers which in the same remayne,
More than we men can fayne,
Poure out your blessing on vs plentiously,
And happy influence vpon vs raine,
That we may raise a large posterity,
Which from the earth, which they may long possesse,
With lasting happinesse,
Vp to your haughty pallaces may mount, 420
And for the guerdon of theyr glorious merit
May heauenly tabernacles there inherit,
Of blessed Saints for to increase the count.
So let vs rest, sweet loue, in hope of this,
And cease till then our tymely joyes to sing,
The woods no more vs answer, nor our eccho ring.

Song made in lieu of many ornaments,
With which my loue should duly haue bene dect,
Which cutting off through hasty accidents,
Ye would not stay your dew time to expect, 430
But promist both to recompens,
Be vnto her a goodly ornament,
And for short time an endlesse moniment.

Notes

Most texts of the *Epithalamion* which appear in modern anthologies are modernized to a considerable degree. The present book provides a text which follows the original (the 1595 octavo volume) except in a very few instances; it will be of service to readers who, for one reason or another, wish to consult an essentially unmodernized version.

Title *Epithalamion* > Greek *epithalamion* (ἐπὶ θάλαμον) > *epi* (near) + *thalamos* (the bridal chamber). Literally, then, a song sung near the bridal chamber. By extension, any song of nuptial celebration. The Latin form was *epithalamium*.

1 *Ye learned sisters:* the Muses, the nine goddesses (daughters of Zeus and Mnemosyne) who inspired the arts and sciences. Spenser begins at once with a phrase whose full allusiveness registers on few readers today. Many of the poet's contemporaries knew their Ovid, however, and would have felt an echo of the Latin writer's "doctae sorores" (*Metamorphoses:* 5. 255; *Fasti:* 6. 811). The adjective *learned* is rich in implications and is a choice of word more characteristic of the Renaissance than of recent times: to the Renaissance poet, writing poetry implied that the poet possessed knowledge and exercised discipline and craftsmanship—in short, was a learned man. To the Renaissance, as to earlier periods, poetry was something nobler than an effusion, an inchoate gush, a means of confession or "self-expression" or self-advertisement.

2 The *others* are illustrious men and women (like Sidney and Ralegh, whom Spenser has celebrated in earlier poems. This reference to a considerable body of earlier poems certainly adds nothing to Douglas Hamer's case that the *Epithalamion* was written, or partly written, much earlier than 1594.

3 By *rymes* Spenser means, of course, poems; *gracefull* means grace-giving or honor-giving.

7–12 The Muses mourn their mishaps in Spenser's *Tears of the Muses* (1591).

12 Spenserian pleonasm: *sorrowfull complaints.*

Epithalamion

12–18   Spenser, like other learned Renaissance poets, is deferent to the genre in which he is writing, and also wants to be sure that his deviations from it are not taken as ignorance or carelessness. His attempt to justify the innovation of writing a nuptial song for himself and his own bride rather than for some other married couple displays both modesty and prudence.

15   *envide:* begrudged

16   Orpheus, the legendary (and possibly to some extent historical) Greek musician and poet *par excellence* who has haunted the imaginations of poets for 3,000 years, bravely went into the underworld and sang so well for Dis that his lovely bride Eurydice was restored to him and would have come into the upper world again had her husband not broken his vow to abstain from looking back at her during their upward journey. However, there is nothing in the myth, or in classical literature, to indicate that Orpheus sang his own *epithalamium.* Perhaps Spenser's line simply refers to the songs Orpheus sang before the rulers of the underworld: would he not have praised Eurydice then?

18   Pastoral refrains similar to this one occur many times in Spenser (e.g. *FQ:* I. VI. 14. 2; *SC:* June, 52).

22   *lusty hed:* vigor

23   Here *bowre* means bedchamber, but the next line enriches the meaning by associating the bedchamber with a bird's nest in a bower of trees.

24   The *love/dove* rhyme was already hackneyed. Shakespeare satirizes it uproariously in *Romeo and Juliet* (c. 1594–5), II. I. 10.

25   Hymen, god who presides at marriage ceremonies; he was traditionally envisioned as bearing a ritual torch (*tead*) at the head of the wedding procession (*maske*).

30   *dight:* dress

33   Usury, or money-lending (usually at high interest rates) was not uncommon in the Middle Ages and in the Renaissance but was condemned by the Church, and Christians were forbidden to practice it. The metaphor is a fine realistic (and somewhat intellectual) touch which helps to balance the high and explicit emotion of the stanza as a whole.

37   The Nymphs are welcome because they are lovely, dainty creatures and were traditionally thought of as artisans with gems and flowers.

that you can heare: poetic syntax for *that can heare you*

44 The ribbon (*riband*) that binds the flowers *trueloue wize* makes the knot that symbolizes the lovers' vow of fidelity.

45 *poses:* posies

51 A meadow (*mead*) is normally patterned or variegated (*diapred*) with many colors (*discolored*).

56 The *Mulla* is the tiny Awbeg River; it flows near Kilcolman Castle (about 25 miles north of Cork), which Spenser first occupied in 1588. *Mulla* is Spenser's derivation from Kilnemullah, an earlier name for the present town of Buttevant, just south of the castle.

carefull heed: Spenserian pleonasm

60 The *rushy lake* refers either to a small lake near the castle or to the lake-like spreading of the Awbeg near Buttevant.

62 Nymphs were usually thought of as having long, flowing hair.

67 The *lightfoot mayds* are forest nymphs, attendants of Artemis (Diana), goddess of the hunt and of chastity.

dere: animals

68 *vse to towre:* climb high

69 The wolves are not fanciful: they prowled County Cork in Spenser's day.

75 *Rosy Morne:* Aurora (goddess of the dawn), married to Tithonus.

77 Phoebus Apollo, god of the sun.

78–84 The chorus of birds is a convention of medieval poetry, as is the conception of them as singing the Mass (cf. Chaucer, *Parliament of Foules* 330–365; G. de Lorris, *Romance of the Rose*, passim).

80 *mattins:* matins, morning (sometimes midnight) prayer in the Roman Catholic Church

81 The mavis too is a thrush.

descant: generally, musical ornamentation or counterpoint; specifically, in plain song, a counterpoint motif sung in a voice higher than that of the cantus firmus (basic melody)

82 *Ouzell:* the blackbird. *Ruddock:* the robin.

87 *make:* (archaic in Spenser's day) mate. Spenser's fondness for archaism and quaint spelling never left him.

95 Hesperus is the evening star.

98 The *fayre houres* are the Horae, the Greek goddesses of the seasons and hence of orderliness generally. Spenser identifies them not only

with the seasons but with the sidereal hours of Ptolemaic astronomy, that is, with the twenty-four 15-divisions of the "sphere of the fixed stars." Time, instead of being conceived as an abstraction, a dimension or medium, is personified and made a causal force: the Hours, because they move (dance, the Elizabethans fancied), regulate (*allot*) the seasons, cause the change from day to night, birth to death, etc.

99   *of:* by

103   The *three handmayds* are the Graces, sister goddesses who attended the Muses. Spenser follows the version of the myth which makes Aglaia (Brilliance), Euphrosyne (Joy), and Thalia (Bloom) attendants of Venus (Aphrodite), the *Cyprian Queene.* Venus was said to have been born on Cyprus.

113   *strayt:* at once

120   *disgrace:* the literal meaning—to take the grace from, to uglify

121   Most writers (including Spenser himself in other poems) name Jove as father of the Muses.

123   *mote:* ought, or could

124   *boone:* wish, request

128   *That:* so that

131   *tabor:* timbrel, small drum; *Croud:* an early form of the fiddle

140   The Latin phrase is a joyous cry to Hymen; *io,* a monosyllable here (yō), is an excited "ah" or "oh."

148   Phoebe is the moon.

151   *seems:* suits

152   *weene:* suppose, think

154   The *golden wyre* simile was a commonplace in medieval and Renaissance verse; Shakespeare satirizes such figures in his Sonnet 130.

155   *perling:* winding

162   *bold:* boldly

165   *Nathlesse:* nevertheless

171–80   In cataloging the beloved's beauties, Spenser is following a tradition that came down to him from ancient and medieval literature.

173   *rudded:* reddened

186   *spright:* spirit, soul

189	*red:* looked at, saw
190	The sight of the matted serpents that formed Medusa's hair turned beholders to stone.
	mazeful: (an extremely rare usage): bewildering, stupefying
196	*base affections:* lower passions
206	*as doth behoue:* as is proper
208	In older usage, a *Saynt* (saint) is any Christian believer.
215–22	Like other Protestant poets, Spenser did not hesitate to describe a Roman Catholic ritual when he wanted to evoke the sense of the poetic and mystical aspects of Christian worship. Milton strongly remembered this passage when he wrote *Il Penseroso* 161–66.
227	*vermill:* vermillion (a bright red)
228	*in grayne:* fast color
234	*sad:* sober, serious
251	The *belly full* means either a full wine-skin or all the guests' bellies will hold.
252	*wull:* want (it)
255	Bacchus, or Dionysus, god of wine and alcoholic revelry and of fertility. The *coronall* is woven of vine or flowers.
261	From the preceding stanza's pagan antiquity we move again into modern Christendom: it was the custom for young Englishmen to take turns ringing the parish bell on wedding days.
262	*wonted:* usual, ordinary
265–6	Because the old (Julian) calendar was ten days behind in Spenser's time, June 11, the feast of St. Barnabas, was the longest day in the year (summer solstice). C. Van Winkle (ed., n., p. 211) quotes the old English proverb: "Barnaby bright, Barnaby bright, / The longest day and the shortest night."
269	In astrology, the sun moves out of the house of the Crab at about mid-June, and so from then on sees the Crab "behind his back."
273	*late:* at last, or at length
281	The conception of Time as having wings is a medievalism; *sad* here means grave or ponderous, rather than sorrowful.
296	*forepast:* previous, past
303	*display:* spread

Epithalamion

304   *Arras:* tapestry

307   Here, as in a number of instances, Spenser takes certain freedoms with the received myths. Maia—the simile is appropriate because this goddess was known for her shyness—lived on Mount Cyllene in Arcadia, not in Tempe (a beautiful valley, sacred to Apollo, in Thessaly), and no one before Spenser had associated her with the Acidalian brook, which the tradition says was sacred to Venus.

316   *defray:* recompense, reimburse

317   *cruell loue:* a stock phrase of Petrarchan or courtly love poetry

318   *for aye:* forever

327   *sad affray:* troubling fright

328   From Jove's seduction of Alcmena, wife of the Theban general Amphitryon, Hercules, *the great Tirynthian groome,* was born—at Tiryns.

330–1   Spenser says that Jove lay with Night and begot Majesty. No source for this lineage has been discovered.

337   *misconceived:* unnecessary, unwarranted

340   *helplesse harmes:* damages past help or remedy

341   By *Ponke* (usually *Pouke* in modern editions) Spenser seems to mean the demon called in Old English *puca;* perhaps the devil.

345   The stork has seldom been regarded as a bird of ill omen; further, it has no voice. Spenser is probably following Chaucer, who (in the *Parliament of Foules,* 361) associates it with marital unfaithfulness.

357   *winged loues:* cupids

374   *Cinthia* is Artemis, who was born on Mount Cynthus. C. Van Winkle (ed., n., p. 121) argues that there is no reference to Queen Elizabeth here.

378   *vnthought:* forgotten

380ff   Cynthia courted the Latmian (>Latmos) shepherd Endymion; it was Pan who (says Virgil in the *Georgics,* III), attracting her with snowy wool, proceeded to assault her. Spenser, exercising his usual freedom, fuses the two stories.

383   *sith:* since, because

390   The lovely goddess Juno was one of the protectors of marriage.

394   *eke:* also (an archaism)

395   *of:* by

398 The pagan Genius was a god of sex and fertility; he was also a guardian spirit who could be invoked to protect a place sacred to him.

405 Hebe, a daughter of Juno, had the power to restore men's youth.

409 The *gods* may be the Judaeo-Christian angels.

414 *fayne:* imagine, conceive

418 *they may:* may they

420 *haughty:* an example of linguistic "degradation"—since Spenser's day, the word has come to connote coldness and snobbishness

421 *guerdon:* treasure, prize

423 Again, not necessarily *canonized* saints.

433 *short time:* the present, the particular time in which we live and which is passing

General

Robert Kellogg and Oliver Steele

Epithalamion: Introduction, *1965**

The *Epithalamion* is Spenser's most conventional and, at the same time, his most original poem. It is also one of a few great lyric poems in English, to be compared in its variety and vitality with Keats' great odes and Wordsworth's *Tintern Abbey*. The form of Spenser's poem is that of the Italian *canzone*, a rare form in English poetry. The *canzone*, as practiced by Dante and Petrarch, consists of a few long stanzas of equal length followed by a short stanza called a *tornata*, which rhetorically is an address to the song just completed. Typically, in Dante and Petrarch, there are five or six long stanzas of thirteen lines in which the predominant five-foot line is varied by one or more three-foot lines. The *tornata* varies from five to seven lines and usually has one short line.[1] Although the *Epithalamion* depends in its form upon the *canzone*, its variations from the Italian models should be noted. Spenser's poem contains twenty-three long stanzas, varying in length from seventeen to nineteen lines; thus both the individual stanzas and the poem are longer than the Italian form, and the varying length of Spenser's stanza contrasts with the regular *canzone* stanza.

If the *Epithalamion* owes something to Dante and Petrarch, it owes still more to Latin poetry and to Catullus particularly. The great *Epithalamium 61* of Catullus is required reading for anyone who wants to understand Spenser's achievement. For the poets of the Renaissance the epithalamia of the Roman poet (61, 62, and 64) are both the be-

---

* From Robert Kellogg and Oliver Steele (eds.), *Edmund Spenser: Books I and II of The Faerie Queene, The Mutability Cantos, and Selections from the Minor Poetry*. New York: The Odyssey Press, 1965, pp. 467–469. Reprinted by permission of the publisher and the author.

[1] See examples of canzone in *The Penguin Book of Italian Verse*, ed. George Kay, pp. 85–88, 91–95, 116–119.

ginning and the supreme models of the marriage song *(epithalamion* can be translated roughly as "on the marriage bed"). In the classical epithalamium two different developments took place. In the first of these, represented by Catullus 64, the development is rather epic than lyric, a song about the loves of gods and heroes, a marriage attended by all Olympus. The second type of epithalamium, represented by Catullus 61, does not lack mythological elements, but its subject is the marriage of real humans. Typically it sings of the dawning of the wedding day, of the festive celebrations, of the beauty of the bride, of the eagerness of the groom. It prays that the union may be fruitful so that the family line may be preserved. Renaissance poets generally chose to follow the first type of epithalamium, perhaps /468/ because of the concern of the age with mythology and because so many renaissance epithalamia were celebrations of marriages between the great aristocratic families of Europe. Spenser chose to follow the second type of epithalamium, partly because his poem was to be more personal and less public than the fully developed mythological type would have allowed, for his song celebrates his own marriage to Elizabeth Boyle in or near Kilcolman, Ireland, in the summer of 1594. No doubt Spenser felt that the epic epithalamium was inappropriate for the marriage of a middle-aged, widowed minor civil servant to the young daughter of an old but not great family. At any rate he chose the more private, more lyrical form and made it his own by mixing with the conventions of the epithalamium as practiced by Catullus and his French renaissance followers details of the Irish locale and folk customs of the English countryside. An even more important transformation of epithalamic convention was accomplished merely by the fact that Spenser decided to celebrate his marriage and praise his young bride by writing his own marriage song; Latin and most renaissance epithalamia had been rather official occasional pieces, written by poets not personally involved in the love they celebrated. If the greatness of the *Epithalamion* is to be explained at all, it may be due to a miraculous blending of the restraints imposed by long literary convention and the fervor of deep personal involvement.

Recently Professor Kent Hieatt has, we think, demonstrated a kind of originality in the *Epithalamion* never suspected before.[2] The basic facts are the following: 1) there are 365 long lines in the poem; 2) the poem is made up of 24 stanzas; 3) night falls, and the refrain changes in the 17th stanza; 4) there is an attempt, by similarities in diction, imagery, and thought, to establish a parallel between stanzas 1–12 and

---

[2] A. Kent Hieatt, *Short Time's Endless Monument*, Columbia University Press, 1960.

stanzas 13–24 (see our notes to stanzas 13–24); and 5) there are 359 long lines in the poem before the *tornata*. Some of these facts are perhaps not surprising. The *Epithalamion* begins at dawn and ends just before dawn the next day. Since it covers a twenty-four hour period, it is appropriate that the poem contain 24 stanzas. However, Spenser's concern to symbolize time and its passage is unusual and intricate. The hours of daylight at the summer solstice (when the wedding took place) in Southern Ireland (where the wedding occurred) were approximately $16\frac{1}{4}$. The refrain of the poem changes in stanza 17, which is divided into four sections by its short lines, and night is said to fall at the end of the first of these sections ($16\frac{1}{4}$). Professor Hieatt argues, in fact, that *Epithalamion* is, in its structure, a symbol of time in all its aspects. The 365 long lines of the poem symbolize the year. The 24 stanzas represent not only the passage of time on Spenser's wedding day, but also the sidereal hours (see note on 98–102), which as Spenser says "allot the seasons." Indeed the various divisions of the 24 stanzas represent the seasons. The first 16 stanzas represent the summer solstice; the 8 following stanzas, the winter solstice, the shortest day; and the two parallel series of stanzas 1–12 and 13–24 represent the two equinoxes of spring and fall. Finally the 359 long lines before the *tornata* are symbolic of the fact that while the sphere of the fixed stars (and the sidereal hours) has completed its 360° east-west orbit, the sun, hanging back, has finished only 359° of its daily orbit. Spenser is saying that when his poem (the sphere of the fixed stars) is over, it /469/ is still not complete (359°). As explained in the note on 98–102, it is this hanging back of the sun that makes the seasons and the year. Professor Hieatt's discovery of the allegory of time in the *Epithalamion* is especially important because, for the first time, it provides a convincing interpretation of the *tornata*. The lines, "Which cutting off through hasty accidents, / Ye would not stay your due time to expect," always a problem before, now become clear. The song, which should have been a perfect ornament—a necklace perhaps—was "cut off" by being finished by the 359th line. Thus it was only an inadequate representation of the sun's orbit, the orbit of the sidereal hours, and the year. The "hasty accidents" are the poem's *accidence,* the sounds and rhythms which make up the poem. The poem would not "stay" its "due time to expect," again because it had come to an end before it has reached completion—360° and 365 days. It had been born before its time. But the *tornata* "recompenses" all of this. It makes a perfect ornament by making symbolically a full circle of the poem. Indeed the *Epithalamion,* celebrating the "short time" of a single day, is an endless monument, symbolizing the ceaseless circles of the sun, the hours, the seasons, and the years.

The modern reader is likely to have some reservations about the elaborate time symbolism of the *Epithalamion*. What has the intricate allegory of time to do with the subject of the poem? How is the marriage of the poet and his young bride related to this allegory? Spenser, in common with most men of his time and of earlier times, saw the life of man as a reflection in little of the operation of the whole of creation. There was the cosmos and then there was man, the *micro*cosm. For both, there was birth and youth (spring), maturity (summer), middle age (fall), and old age and death (winter). As the ceaseless revolutions of the stars and the planets usher in a continual round of change, making an eternity of endless mutability; so men and women, themselves creatures of change, create in marriage a kind of eternity by bringing children to life, children who, in their turn, will continue the life of the microcosm. Furthermore, human love and marriage create another kind of eternity of the merely temporary stuff of earthly life, for the children, who are the end of marriage and who guarantee the preservation of life within time, may inherit a true eternity outside of time. Their souls are immortal and they may die to live forever in heaven. The allegory of time, then, is a passionate exaltation of married love as the means by which imperfect, changeful mortals make eternity.

A modern reader, however, is likely to object in principle to this kind of symbolism as being external to the poem, or inorganic. What is organic in the literature of any time will depend partly upon what is organic in the life and thought of the time—what experiences, sensations, ideas are seen to be obviously or naturally or reasonably related in a coherent structure of belief and action. All that one can say is that the symbolism of time which informs the *Epithalamion* was part of such a coherent structure, in which marriage, sexual love, time, and eternity seemed obviously and naturally related. This answer may not modify anyone's reservations much, but perhaps an entirely satisfactory answer on this point is not necessary to an appreciation of the poem. Keats', Yeats' and Eliot's reasons for loving the *Epithalamion* are perfectly good ones. The marvelous variety of effects, in rhythm, in language, in tone, is satisfaction enough.

C. S. Lewis

From English Literature in the Sixteenth Century, Excluding Drama, *1954**

The *Epithalamium* is our only evidence that Spenser, had he chosen, might have been among the very greatest lyrical poets: lyrical, of course, after the manner of Pindar, not that of Herrick or Burns. The song, as practised by Wyatt, was a form which he either never attempted or attempted so unsuccessfully that he destroyed the result; his talents did not lie in that direction. But for the Greater Ode he had powers unequalled in English.[1] The *Epithalamium*, despite its Italian and Latin affinities, is the most Pindaric thing we have. It has one, or perhaps two, faults; the refrain loses some of its beauty when, at line 333, it has to pass into the negative, and the choir of frogs that make us 'wish theyr choking' is either too comic or else not comic enough. All /373/ the rest is, I think, perfection, and here, if nowhere else, the Drab has been completely purged away. The resemblance to Pindar lies in the festal sublimity (a thing much rarer than tragic sublimity) and in the triumphant fusion of many different elements. The Bacchanalian or fescennine jollity of the fourteenth strophe, the hushed sensuousness of the seventeenth, the grotesque night fears of the nineteenth, the realism of 'Those trouts and pikes all others doo excell', and the transformation whereby a small Protestant church becomes a Salomonic or even a pagan temple and at the same time a great cathedral of the old religion with high altar, roaring organs, and crowds of hovering angels, are very different and drawn from different traditions. What organizes them all is the steady progression of the bridal day. Catullus began with evening: thus losing all the alacrity of Spenser's earlier

---

* From C. S. Lewis, *English Literature in the Sixteenth Century, Excluding Drama*. Oxford: Clarendon Press, 1954, pp. 372-73. Reprinted by permission of the publisher and the author.

[1] Except, perhaps, by Hopkins and Charles Williams.

strophes with their 'Awake', 'Bid her awake', 'Hymen is awake', 'The wished day is come at last'. Joy does not begin to pass into 'merriment' (with a medieval chorus of birds) till strophe five. The suggestion of heat (it is high summer) is delayed till seven. At the same time the emotional development is artfully varied and interrupted as in a good symphony. The lustiness which breaks out fully in fourteen had been just hinted by the 'strong confused noyse' in eight and then hushed by the processional movement of the five that follow. The moonlight in twenty-one comes as unexpectedly as a new turn in a novel or play. The intense desire for posterity (who will people not only earth but heaven) and the astrological connexion of this with the 'thousand torches flaming bright' above the house-tops add not only a public but almost a cosmic solemnity to the poem; which remains, none the less, a thoroughly personal love poem—'Let this day let this one day be myne'—with a remembrance of 'sorrowes past'.

In the *Prothalamium* (1596) his success was not so complete. The central structural idea, that of the swans' gliding progress down the river, is a happy one, and the refrain is more emotionally relevant than the refrain of the *Epithalamium*. But I cannot feel that perfect unity has been achieved. The references to Spenser's own discontents, to the history of the Temple, and to the achievements of Essex, interesting as they are in themselves, do not seem to have been made to contribute much to the total effect. And there is perhaps a little awkwardness at the end of the sixth strophe.

Émile Legouis

From Spenser, *1926**

The poem is remarkable, not so much for originality in treatment of the subject, as for its copious and inexhaustible flow, for the alacrity with which Spenser catches up all his reminiscences of traditional poetry to adorn his beloved with them and magnify the real circumstances and homely details of a wedding which took place in a small seaport of Ireland, Cork or Youghal, on the 11th of June, 1594.

Even in his most personal poems, where he expresses his feelings most directly—the *Epithalamion* and *Amoretti*—Spenser's genius for idealising his subject remains apparent. Though he sings the praises of his bride, he offers us the picture, not so much of a distinct and individual woman, as of the typical woman on the bridal day. His beloved is perfectly beautiful; none of the features of conventional beauty are wanting to her portrait—her complexion like a blend of lilies and roses, her /95/ fair-coloured hair, her blue eyes: she is the young girl, all blushes, all modesty and shamefastness—without a single irregularity in her looks or person, without one jarring note in the absolute harmony of her perfection. Spenser has surely, according to his promise, made her immortal, but one may wonder whether he has made her truly *live*. It is his own ecstasy and rapture, his lifelong adoration of feminine beauty that he sings at his wedding-time, in a few exquisite sonnets, and in this, the most superb epithalamion that has ever been written.

---

* From Émile Legouis, *Spenser*. London and Toronto: J. M. Dent and Sons, 1926, pp. 94–95. Reprinted by permission of the publisher and the author.

J. W. Mackail

From The Springs of Helicon, *1909**

The Epithalamion, in Johnson's stately phrase of compliment, "it were vain to blame, and useless to praise." For sustained beauty of execution, for melodiousness in which the most melodious of English poets excels even his own standard, for richness of ornament that stops just short of excess, and does not either blur the outline or clog the movement, it easily takes the first place, not only among Spenser's own lyrics, but among all English odes. The mechanism of the verse is /103/ a marvel of delicate intricacy. The twenty-three long undulating stanzas into which it is divided by the recurrent but perpetually varying refrain are all based on the same general rhythmical scheme of subdivision, but with variations of internal srtucture devised with extreme skill to prevent monotony, to give the play and freedom of a live organism.

---

* From J. W. Mackail, *The Springs of Helicon.* London: Longmans, Green, and Co., 1909, pp. 102–103. Reprinted by permission of the publisher and the author.

Cortlandt Van Winkle

From Epithalamion (Introduction), *1926**

Spenser /10/ is the poet par excellence who has restored to the wedding-hymn mention of popular customs and beliefs. So well blended are his Irish and English folk-lore with the classical machinery of pagan hymenaia that we note no incongruity, nor do we question its appropriateness. Rather does the folk-lore help to vivify and heighten the personal and subjective character of the *Epithalamion* and make more real his wedding sung so joyfully by the Poet. Whether Spenser knew it or not—I believe it to be one of those happy intuitions which ever flash out from a man of genius in his moments of greater inspiration—he drew very near to the spirit of pre-Homeric, pre-Hesodian, pre-Sapphic epithalamists, and his poem stands first among literary products of the genre to recapture popular spirit and mirror, if but for a moment, the hopes and fears of the people.

---

* From Cortlandt Van Winkle, *Epithalamion* (Introduction). New York: F. S. Crofts & Co., 1926, pp. 9–10. Reprinted by permission of the publisher and the author.

Origins, Genre

Thomas M. Greene

Spenser and the Epithalamic Convention*

When Spenser wrote his *Epithalamion* in 1594, he was acutely conscious that his poem was conventional—that is, that it stood in a given relationship to certain past poems and, once published, would be assimilated with them in their relationship to future poems. His conception of past epithalamia was different from his conception, for example, of the sources of the *Prothalamion,* a title which he invented. He would have been aware, moreover, that not all poems for weddings were epithalamia, and that not even all the poems entitled "Epithalamion" fitted strictly into the convention. I shall here sketch briefly the history of the genre, describe the convention as Spenser received it, and attempt to show what in his poem is conventional and what is not, adding interpretative comments that seem relevant.

Although descriptions of a wedding procession involving songs appear in Homer (*Iliad*, XVIII) and Hesiod (*The Shield of Herakles*), the ancestry of the epithalamic convention goes back to Sappho.[1] There is evidence that earlier Greek poets, such as Hesiod and Alcman, wrote nuptial poems; but Sappho's fragments are the earliest which have survived. Brief nuptial songs appear in Aristophanes' *Peace* and *The Birds,* and in other Greek plays, but the next true epithalamion is the

---

* From *Comparative Literature*, IX (Summer, 1957), 215–28. Reprinted by permission of the editors and the author.

[1] Psalm 45 (in the Vulgate Psalm 44) is also an epithalamion, apparently for a royal wedding. Given the distance between Hebrew culture and Greek culture, there is a surprising number of elements which the psalm has in common with the convention known to Spenser. Although contemporary scholars do not consider the *Song of Songs* to have been written for a wedding, early in the Christian era it was interpreted as a celebration of an allegorical marriage. Spenser drew upon the *Song of Songs* (see Israel Baroway, "The Imagery of Spenser and the Song of Songs," *Journal of English and Germanic Philology*, XXXIII, 1934, 23), but it was not widely influential in the Renaissance, perhaps because it was considered to be too sacred.

eighteenth eclogue of Theocritus, written for the wedding of Helen and Menelaus.

Latin poets adopted the genre but did not immediately alter it radically. Catullus introduced native wedding customs into the first of his three nuptial poems, the beautiful *Epithalamium* (No. 61) for Vinia Aurunculeia and Manlius Torquatus, the single most influential poem of antiquity upon the Renaissance epithalamists. His other two nuptial poems are No. 62, the *Carmen Nuptiale*, a much briefer song in the form of a dialogue between choruses of youths and maidens, written for no specific occasion, and No. 64, a long narrative *epyllion* written for the legendary wedding of Peleus and Thetis. After Catullus, Ovid is said /216/ to have written an epithalamion which has been lost; the first chorus of Seneca's tragedy *Medea* may be based upon it.

With the *Epithalamium in Stellam et Violentillam* of Statius (written about A.D. 90), the genre entered a new stage which was to influence the Renaissance far less than the Sapphic-Catullan type (to be described below). Statius' poem, which was imitated by Claudian and several other late Latin epithalamists, consisted of a rather wooden mythological narrative centering around Venus and Cupid. After Statius, the only interesting nuptial poetry is found in the lyrical *Fescennina* which precede one of Claudian's two formal epithalamia. Interest in the genre may have been stimulated in late antiquity by rhetoricians such as Dionysius of Halicarnassus, Menander, Himerius, and Choricius of Gaza, who wrote prescriptions for or examples of wedding orations. In the Middle Ages Latin devotional poems entitled *Epithalamium* were written, but they had virtually nothing in common with the classical genre.

In the fifteenth century the genre was revived by neo-Latin poets and became so familiar that it could be satirized playfully by Erasmus in his *Colloquia* ("Epithalamium Petri Aegidii"). The best of the fifteenth-century epithalamists was Giovanni Pontano, who wrote nuptial poems, among others, for the marriages of two daughters. The practice of writing neo-Latin epithalamia was carried on by Ariosto and lasted through most of the sixteenth century; the best-known examples are the atypical erotic poem of Johannes Secundus and the patriotic celebration of Mary Stuart's first marriage by the Scottish poet George Buchanan.[2]

The genre was neglected by quattrocento poets writing in Italian.

---

[2] For texts, see Giovanni Gioviano Pontano, *Carmina*, ed. Soldati (Florence, 1902) II, 160, 164; Ludovico Ariosto, *Lirica*, ed. Fatini (Bari, 1924), p. 217; Johannes Secundus, *Les Baisers* (Latin text ed. and trans. Maurice Rat, Paris, 1938), p. 36; D. A. Millar, ed., *George Buchanan: A Memorial* (St. Andrews, 1907), p. 300.

Torquato Tasso may have been correct in stating that a poem written by his father Bernardo in 1531 was the earliest in the language, although the primacy is hard to establish with certainty.[3] Examples can be found in anthologies such as Domeniche's *Delle rime di diversi nobilissimi et eccellentissimi autori* (Venice, 1550) and Atanagi's *De le rime di diversi nobili poeti toscani* (Venice, 1565). The genre really flowered in Italy, however, only with Tasso and Marino, neither of whom was truly conventional. Tasso wrote no formal "epitalamio," but he did write thirteen nuptial poems entitled simply "Nelle nozze di. . ." /217/ or "Per le nozze di. . ." These poems did not adhere strictly to the traditional Catullan pattern but borrowed elements freely from that pattern. One of them, written for the wedding of Marfisa d'Este with her cousin Alfonsino, has been ranked among Tasso's finest lyrics.[4] Marino wrote ten epithalamia which differed greatly among themselves in structure and style and which represented even more of a break with the Catullan convention than Tasso's poems.

In France the history of the genre, in vernacular language, really begins with Ronsard, although Eustache Deschamps had written two nuptial *ballades,* and Marot two genial and intimate poems for the marriages of royal princesses.[5] Marot's poems contain occasional borrowings from Catullus, but in tone as well as content they are worlds away from the convention. Ronsard's *Epithalame* (written in 1548), on the other hand, clearly falls within the convention, though it depends more on Theocritus than on Catullus. It was published in Book IV of the *Odes* and prepared the way for a flood of other epithalamia. All but one of the Pléiade poets (Pontus de Tyard) wrote epithalamia, as did most of the other court poets. Among the wealth of examples, Belleau's delicate, lyrical celebration of the princess Claude's wedding in 1558 stands out as particularly attractive. The long *Epithalame* in dramatic form by Du Bellay for the wedding of Marguerite de France, sister of Henry II, is another important example.[6] The convention remained more or less intact in France to the end of the century. In the new literary atmosphere it was virtually abandoned in nuptial poems

---

[3] In one of his *Discorsi del poema eroico* T. Tasso alluded to his father's poem as "il Epitalamio fatto nelle nozze del Duca Federico, il quale fu peravventura il primo, che si legesse in questa lingua" (*Opere,* ed. Rosini, Pisa, 1821–32, XII, 16). For the text of this poem see Bernardo Tasso, *De gli Amori* (Venice, 1555), p. 197.

[4] See Augusto Sainati, *La lirica di Torquato Tasso* (Pisa, 1912).

[5] Eustache Deschamps, *Oeuvres inédites* (Paris, 1849), I, 154, II, 6, Clément Marot, *Oeuvres,* ed. Yve-Plessis and Plattard (Paris, 1875–1931), V, 85, 98.

[6] Pierre de Ronsard, *Oeuvres complètes,* ed. Laumonier (Paris, 1914–49), I, 9. Rémy Belleau, *Oeuvres poétiques,* ed. Marty-Laveaux (Paris, 1878), I, 238. Joachim du Bellay, *Oeuvres poétiques,* ed. Chamard (Paris, 1908–31), V, 201.

by Bertaut and Malherbe, and finally parodied out of existence by the zestful indecencies of Scarron.

In England there are few examples before Spenser; after Spenser the genre has an intricate history. Although at least two earlier poets, Lydgate and Dunbar, wrote nuptial poems, Sidney's *Epithalamion* sung by Dicus in the third eclogue of the *Arcadia* was the first of its kind. Its composition may possibly have been antedated by a translation by Bartholomew Young of a Spanish poem drawn from Gil Polo's continuation of Montemayor's pastoral romance *Diana*. These are the only two English epithalamia which preceded Spenser's poem, and it is interesting that they are both pastorals. The list of seventeenth-century English poets who wrote epithalamia is a long and distinguished one including Donne, Jonson, Herrick, Crashaw, Marvell, and Dryden.[7] /218/ Indeed, to follow the progress of the genre is to follow in microcosm the development of seventeenth-century English poetry. It is remarkable that Spenser's poem did not exhaust the epithalamion in England but seems rather to have given it fresh impetus.

The genre acquired increased status in the Renaissance by the discussion devoted to it in such rhetorical treatises as Scaliger's *Poetices* and Puttenham's *Arte of English Poesie*.[8] These discussions combined historical references to past models with rules governing the genre itself. The characteristics most essential to the Renaissance epithalamic convention are the following:

(1) The principals of the wedding celebrated, when it is not fictive, usually belong to the nobility (this is less true in England than on the continent). The poet of course need not be well born himself but he is with few exceptions financially dependent upon the upper class. The weddings which are distinguished enough to be celebrated in verse are the weddings of people wealthy enough to reward the poet and prominent enough socially or politically to justify, so to speak, his encomia. It follows as a corollary of this patron-poet relationship that the epithalamion must contain praise of the bride and bridegroom. Spenser, himself formerly patronized by noblemen, was so conscious of the comparative social obscurity of his own marriage that the first stanza of

---

[7] The standard, although incomplete, anthology of English epithalamia is edited by Robert H. Chase, *English Epithalamies* (London, 1896). There are two German dissertations which discuss this material: Kurt Wohrmann, *Die englische Epithalamiendichtung der Renaissance und ihre Vorbilder* (Leipzig, 1928); Adelheid Gaertner, *Die englische Epithalamienliteratur im siebzehnten Jahrhundert und ihre Vorbilder* (Coburg, 1936). The best edition of Spenser's *Epithalamion* is by Cortlandt Van Winkle (New York, 1926).

[8] Julius Caesar Scaliger, *Poetices* (Heidelberg, 1617). George Puttenham, *Arte of English Poesie*, ed. Willcock-Walker (Cambridge, 1936).

his poem announces the reversal of the traditional relationship: "So I unto myself alone will sing." There are a few instances in which the principals belong to the upper middle class. In these cases, shifts in tone and treatment—a curtailment of flattery, greater freedom of allusion, etc.—are usually apparent at once.

(2) The epithalamion must follow classical models, in particular Catullus' No. 61. The specific nature of this influence will be described below. First, however, the functioning of the influence should be understood in terms of literary convention. As the body of Renaissance epithalamia increased, the influence of any single poem decreased; in place of the poem, the epithalamist drew upon a stockpile of *topoi*, commonplaces, similes, epithets, traditional good wishes, common strategies and techniques. The epithalamist seems to have been aware of the genre, not so much as a number of individual poems among which he could choose his own "source," but rather as a body of poetic material which was itself intricately entangled with borrowings and /219/ derivation, a body from which he could draw without necessarily incurring a debt to a given poem. Attempts have been made by scholars to link Spenser's epithalamion to a specific source.[9] But for a student of the convention all such attempts break down because any given *topos* found in Spenser can be found in several earlier epithalamia.

One might define a convention as a set of allusions. A convention exists when the full literary meaning of a word or a line requires a knowledge of many past works in order to be wholly understood. The vocabulary of a pastoral elegy or a Petrarchan sonnet requires a familiarity with comparable works for its allusiveness to be appreciated. It follows that the first example one encounters in a convention cannot be read as the poet expected his work to be read.

(3) The epithalamion implies a social context. It assumes always a wedding attended by guests participating in a commonly shared jubilation. For a wedding without these elements the epithalamion would have to invent them. Apparently the poem was often a literal part of the entertainment accompanying the ceremony, comparable to the music, singing, dancing, and masques which the greatest weddings required.

(4) The epithalamion must refer to a specific day, fictive or real. Poems containing only generalized good wishes for the wedded couple are not epithalamia. To be conventional the poem must be constructed

---

[9] Wohrmann, *op. cit.*, links it with Catullus' No. 61. James A. S. McPeek, in *Catullus in Strange and Distant Britain* (Cambridge, 1939), links it with several "sources" but, particularly Marc Claude Buttet's *Epithalame aux nosses de très magnanime prince Emmanuel Philibert de Savoie*...

around the events of the wedding day itself—the religious rites, the banqueting, the bedding of bride and bridegroom (itself a ritual), and the sexual consummation. Thus the poem acquires dramatic impetus not from an institution—marriage—but from a series of concrete actions—a wedding. Aristotle, in the *Rhetoric* (I,3), distinguished ceremonial or epideictic rhetoric from political and judicial in that the first treated of the present, the second of the future, and the third of the past. The epithalamist imitates the classical epideictic orator in assuming the occasion to be at hand.

In antiquity the successive stages of the wedding festivities provided various pretexts for song. There was a song for the wedding procession, a song for the bedding of the couple, the morning song for their reawakening the next day. The word "epithalamion," derived from the Greek *thalamos*, "bed chamber," implies that it was originally only one of these kinds of wedding poems. The Greek generic name for all these songs was *hymenaios*.

(5) The epithalamion involves the fictive poet-speaker in a certain complex and highly stylized role. This role is one of the most distinctive /220/ and interesting features of the epithalamic convention. A. L. Wheeler, in *Catullus and the Traditions of Ancient Poetry*, makes the following remarks on the role assumed by Catullus in his epithalamion for Manlius Torquatus (No. 61):

> The Greek element appears most prominently however in matters of technique. The most interesting feature here is the mimetic-dramatic character of the poem—the manner in which the poet represents himself as taking part in the ceremony in the role of a master of ceremonies and chorus leader. It is the poet who invokes Hymen, urges the girls to sing, addresses the bride, apostrophizes the wedding couch, directs the boys to lift their torches and sing, addresses the favorite slave, the groom—all the persons in fact. Sometimes he maintains his individuality . . . sometimes he associates himself with the rest of the company . . . This is the device which more than anything else gives life to the poem. No other completely extant wedding poem is composed in this way, but the same technique is employed in other forms of poetry, for example in the *Hymns* of Callimachus.[10]

Wheeler is right in saying that no other extant wedding poem of antiquity is written from this assumed role, but there is evidence that Catullus's chief source, Sappho, assumed a role which resembled her imitator's. The evidence is contained in an exemplary wedding oration

---

[10] A. L. Wheeler, *Catullus and the Traditions of Ancient Poetry* (Berkeley, 1934), p. 200.

by Himerius, a Greek rhetorician of late antiquity (315–381 B.C.). In his *Oration for the Marriage of Severus* he recalls the epithalamia of Sappho and says of them:

> It is she [Sappho] who after the mock combats enters the bridal precincts, decorates the room, spreads the couch, marshals the maidens into the bridal chamber, brings Aphrodite in her car of Graces, and a bevy of Loves to play with her. She twines the bride's hair with hyacinths ... but the wings of the Loves and their locks she decks with gold, and dispatches them before the car as an escort waving their torches on high.[11]

This description of the poetess' commanding part in the wedding festivities seems to relate directly to what impresses Wheeler in Catullus' poem. One may conclude from Himerius' evocation that like Catullus Sappho made of herself a kind of mistress of ceremonies, presiding over each successive scene of the wedding pageant and seeming to control its evolution by invocations, apostrophes, and commands. There can be little doubt that Catullus' own mimetic role derives from Sappho.

During the Renaissance the role was accepted almost universally by epithalamists. It is the poet-speaker who makes the wedding arrangements and in the act writes his poem. In some inferior poems he is almost officious, despite his determined high spirits: the chorus of maidens must be out of bed; the correct gods must attend with the correct gifts; the roistering must not prevent the couple from retiring; the sun must not slow his pace; the bride must not be too fearful /221/ nor the bridegroom too impetuous. Most epithalamia, like Spenser's, are written chiefly in the second person and in the optative subjunctive. The poet-speaker acts as an advocate for society, assuring the couple that they are fortunate, that they are doing wisely to marry, wishing them the socially valuable blessings of prosperity, harmony, and increase. As a result the typical epithalamion is a ritualistic *public* statement, unconcerned with the actual intimate experience undergone by individuals.

The commands, invocations, flattery, and optatives of the speaker all function to call into being the ideal event which the wedding must be, the ideal as defined partly by the convention, partly by the particular society, partly by the poet. A wedding is an ambiguous enough event to permit many interpretations. Something has happened when the wedding day and night are past, but epithalamists do not agree on the

---

[11] Quoted in *Sappho—Poems and Fragments*, ed. and trans. C. R. Haines (London, 1926), p. 52.

nature of the happening. It may be primarily a sexual event, but it may be also a social event, a religious event, or, at the highest level, a political event. It may even in certain poems be related to the natural macrocosmos and thus become a kind of cosmic event. The epithalamist is able to define the event which has occurred through the commands and injunctions which he chooses to make, through the various actions of the wedding day and night which he chooses to name and evoke. Almost all epithalamia include the bedding of the bride and bridegroom, but even this can be treated in widely different terms.

The underlying optative pressure exerted by the poem, the pressure of the ideal conception upon the actual occasion, is felt throughout. Kenneth Burke has discussed the "magical" use of language as decree.[12] This is the characteristic use of language in the epithalamion. It becomes explicit in the concluding *allocutio sponsalis*, where the couple is addressed directly and the traditional wishes are made for their future, typically in the optative subjunctive.

An eighteenth-cenutry critic wrote this of the genre: "Le but de l'Epithalame est de faire connoître aux nouveaux époux le bonheur de leur union, par les louanges qu'on leur donne successivement, et par les avantages qu'on leur annonce pour l'avenir."[13] To announce to the newly married the happiness of their union—a rhetorical function is involved here which Aristotle, in two separate passages,[14] distinguishes /222/ from praise, a function which most Aristotelian translators render as "felicitation" or "gratulation" but which a more courageous translator, W. D. Ross, has rendered, lamely and accurately, as "calling happy."[15] One may recall Dryden: "O happy, happy, happy pair!" The Greek term for this is *makarismos*. The epithalamion can be regarded as a series of invocations to action which will demonstrate the ideal felicity of the wedding and thus function as *makarismos*.

With this background we may turn to Spenser's poem, the one epithalamion besides Catullus' which ranks with the world's great poems.

---

[12] Kenneth Burke, *The Philosophy of Literary Form* (Baton Rouge, 1941).

[13] Abbé Souchay, "Discours sur l'origine et le caractère de l'épithalame," in *Académie Royal des Inscriptions et Belles Letters*, IX (1736), 305.

[14] "To call any one blest is, it may be added, the same thing as to call him happy; but these are not the same thing as to bestow praise and encomium upon him; the two latter are a part of 'calling happy,' just as goodness is a part of happiness." *Rhetoric*, I, 9. "Clearly what applies to the best things is not praise, but something greater and better, as is indeed obvious; for what we do to the gods and the most godlike of men is to call them blessed and happy." *Nicomachean Ethics*, I, 12.

[15] Compare also Hobbes: "The form of speech whereby men signify their opinion of the goodness of any thing, is *Praise*... And that whereby they signify the opinion they have of a man's felicity, is by the Greeks called *Makarismos*, for which we have no name in our tongue." *Leviathan*, ed. Oakeshott (Oxford, 1955), p. 39.

The conventional elements noted above are all present in Spenser, with the exception of the aristocratic milieu. Many conventional *topoi*, moreover, appear in Spenser: among others, the "maske" of Hymen; the attendance of the Graces upon the bride; the praise of the bride's beauty; the impatience with the tardy sun; the greeting of Hesperus; the bedding of the bridal couple, with the injunction to break off the revelry; the concluding invocations which replace the *allocutio sponsalis*.

In the remaining pages of this article I shall discuss ways in which Spenser developed, modified, and broke with the convention. His first original stroke was to fuse the roles of bridegroom and poet-speaker; to my knowledge no epithalamist had ever done this before. In most respects the device is successful; it makes perfect sense in the poem and confers added motivation for the speaker's injunctions and directions. His invocation to the Muses, nymphs, and Graces who wait upon his bride can be read as tokens of his solicitious regard for her. His praise of her inner and outer beauty in stanzas nine through eleven appear as spontaneous expressions of his love. His command "Pour out the wine..." is reasonable because he is the host. And the concluding prayerful invocations gain a particular fervency because they are prayers for the speaker's own marriage.

These invocations are striking examples of Spenser's fine moral taste. One may compare them with the *allocutio* of the *Prothalamion*, which is highly conventional, albeit the only conventional stanza of the poem:

> Joy may you have, and gentle hearts content
> Of your loves couplement;
> And let faire Venus, that is Queene of love,
> With her heart-quelling Sonne upon you smile,
> Whose smile, they say, hath vertue to remove
> All Loves dislike, and friendships faultie guile
> For ever to assoile. /223/
> Let endlesse Peace your steadfast hearts accord,
> And blessed Plentie wait upon your bord;
> And let your bed with pleasures chast abound,
> That fruitful issue may to you afford,
> Which may your foes confound,
> And make your joyes redound
> Upon your Brydale day, which is not long...

In the *Epithalamion* Spenser refrains significantly from asking for joy or conjugal pleasure. He assumes them and does not insult his bride by asking for them. He does refer to Genius who, he says, ensures conjugal chastity and pleasure, but he specifically asks him only for offspring. This is, in fact, the chief gift he asks of all the gods invoked. For his offspring he asks happiness but not the other conventional gifts —fame, heroism, and fertility—nor does he ask that they "confound" his foes; he asks rather that they be permitted untimate sainthood in Heaven. There are no references in the *Epithalamion* to envy or jealousy, "Loves dislike, and friendships faultie guile," the besetting evils of marriage which were frequently exorcised. These would also be in bad taste where the bridegroom is his own petitioner.

It is only the consummation itself which presents an insuperable problem in tact to the bridegroom-speaker. Spenser, with his delicacy and reverence for his bride, could not have permitted himself any license which would be acceptable from a third person. His solution was to divert attention to the ornamental Cupids playing about the bed, a solution not entirely satisfactory. An emotional vacuum is almost created at the point where conventionally emotions are highest. The emotional climax is reserved for the concluding prayers.

The fusion of the bridegroom and speaker roles is not the only original element in the poem. The unconventionality of the bourgeois milieu has already been noted, but some corollary consequences of this might be pointed out. First of all it is interesting that Spenser insists upon rather than veils the provinciality of the occasion. There is a distinctly bourgeois pleasure in the "silken courteins," "odourd sheetes, and Arras coverlets" of the bridal bed, a pleasure which would be unseemly at an aristocratic occasion. The bourgeois world is represented most vividly by the merchant's daughters who watch the bridal procession and attend the feast. The effect of their mediocrity is to render the bride more brilliant. There is a lively humor in the poet's patronizing manner to them, his questioning whether they have ever seen anyone so fair, and why they forget to sing when they see her:

> And stand astonisht lyke to those which red
> Medusaes mazeful hed.

Later in the church they are admonished to learn obedience and humility /224/ from the bride. It is they finally who are enjoined to bring the bride to her chamber, breaking off their sports and ceasing to sing.

> Enough it is, that all the day was youres.

They are associated with the daytime world of activity and festivity which is no longer becoming after the arrival of darkness. With the welcome to night and silence, they disappear from the poem. Conventionally the bride was usually attended by handmaids, but these were never truly realized dramatically.

The bourgeois milieu permits a release of humor which would have been unseemly in the conventional epithalamion. There are a dozen touches of delicate comedy sprinkled through the poem, evidence of the jocularity befitting one's own wedding day. There is the impatient bridegroom's assurance to the sun that his "tired steeds long since have need of rest," a witty way of handling an old *topos*. There is the description of the angels at church who forget to worship out of wonder at the bride's beauty. There is the admonition to the nymphs of Mulla to bind up their hair in order to look their best. There is the wry and realistic allusion to the croking "Quire of Frogs," a reminder of the boggy Irish countryside. There is the tardy regret that the longest rather than the shortest day of the year was chosen for the wedding. There is the admonition to the young men of the town to write down the date lest they forget it. There is even the punning play on "consent" when Spenser avers that the birds, by their harmonious song

> all agree, with sweet consent,
> To this dayes merriment.

These benign and gentle touches represent perhaps the closest approach of the Renaissance epithalamion to the vulgar Fescennine jokes of antiquity.

Another unconventional element lies in Spenser's use of his stanza form. The intricate form was derived by Spenser from the Italian *canzone*, although no Italian poem has been found composed in the identical pattern. Italian epithalamia, including Tasso's nuptial poems, were commonly written in the form of *canzoni*, but of course the form was not limited to epithalamia. Spenser's stanza is unusual in its length, varying as it does from seventeen to nineteen lines, and in its number of recurrences. There are twenty-three stanzas in the *Epithalamion*, whereas the typical Italian *canzone* does not exceed eight or ten. The concluding brief address to the poem, the envoy, was characteristic of the *canzone* and was called technically a *tornata* or *commiato*. On the whole the *canzone* as written by Italian poets tended to be a more static poem than Spenser's. The length and complexity of the stanza tended to strengthen the autonomy of each unit and to render the concluding /225/ line more of a conclusion. Spenser's refrain, which is not a characteristic of the *canzone*, renders the conclusion even more emphatic. Thus to write in this form with so strong a narrative element—for the *Epithalamion* is in fact a kind of story—was to demonstrate an audacity of which few Italian poets would have been capable. Spenser's use of the canzone was a deformation of its spirit and of its apparent technical limitations.[16]

It has been said that these limitations were in fact too great for Spenser. John Erskine, for example, wrote:

> Strictly speaking, each stanza, with its own inspiration, is a song in itself, and the complete poem is a series rather than an organic whole. But the lyrical emotion aroused by all motives is the same in every case, so that, in the broad sense, it would be difficult to deny unity to the poem.[17]

But it is demonstrably untrue that the emotion of all the stanzas is alike; one has only to compare the fourteenth stanza—"Pour out the wine without restraint or stay"—with the last. Actually the poem is remarkable for its sudden shifts of tone and mood.

If it is true that the poem is only a series of distinct stanzas, then the poem is certainly a failure. Undeniably the individual stanzas of the *Epithalamion*, more than those of most poems, do have a heightened autonomy; the prosodic variations in length and pattern among them tend to increase their distinctiveness. Each makes a fresh beginning; each evolves with a certain spontaneity; each reaches its foreknown conclusion with renewed ingenuity. But to say this is not to admit that the relationship between the stanzas is factitious. The reader is insensitive who does not feel the balance and architecture of the parts, the calculated progression of feeling, the movement forward to a culmination.[18] /226/

---

[16] Spenser may have been influenced by the Sidney or the Polo-Young epithalamion. Both of these were written in an identical uneven stanza with refrain; neither, however, could be called a *canzone*.

[17] John Erskine, *The Elizabethan Lyric* (New York, 1903), p. 189.

[18] I am tempted to find more elaborate structural balance than other students have discovered. It has been pointed out that, if the prefatory first stanza is disregarded, the two stanzas describing the church ceremony are exactly central; ten stanzas precede and ten follow. I am inclined to see an ulterior division into three-four-three stanzas of each of these groups of ten. The first group of three consists of injunctions to the Muses and nymphs to attend the bride at her waking. The next group of four, beginning with the line, "Wake now, my love, awake; for it is time," concerns the preparations for the day. The next group of three, beginning with stanza nine, consists of three descriptions of the bride, evoking in turn her immediate beauty as a bride, her physical bodily beauty, and her inner Platonic beauty. After the service three stanzas carry us from the ceremony to nightfall. The seventeenth stanza, beginning "Now ceasse, ye damsels, your delights fore-past ... Now day is doen, and night is nighing fast," clearly marks a new beginning, and this is emphasized by the shift in the refrain. Stanzas seventeen through twenty form the night group, which is set off significantly from the preceding daylight stanzas; this group ends the narrative proper. The last three consist of prayerful invocations to the gods.

Unity is also gained by imagistic motifs which recur frequently enough to be significant. Spenser adopted conventional *topoi*, extended and modified them, and added original inventions of his own to form these harmonious and elegant patterns of description and allusion. Jones[19] has discussed the auditory imagery of the poem, imagery which the refrain requires and emphasizes. Spenser's mastery appears here in the deft suiting of sound to mood at each hour of the day, in the choice of images which echo but also help to create personal emotion. One is also struck by the imagery of light and darkness, an antithesis associated with other antitheses of day and night, harmonious or boisterous sound and precarious silence, rising and dressing on the one hand and retiring and undressing on the other.

The poem is unconventional in the repeated expression it gives to the ominous elements associated with night, the elements which might potentially destroy the joy of the wedding and even the marriage. The induction refers to mishaps raised by "death or love or fortune's wreck?" in the lives of those who have appeared earlier in Spenser's poem. The second stanza refers to the vicissitudes of the courtship dramatized in the *Amoretti*, the "pains and sorrows past," and the Muses are asked to sing of "solace" as well as of joy to the bride. At nightfall the appearance of Hesperus, a *topos* which goes back to Sappho, occasions unconventional praise of the star for its guidance of lovers "through the nights sad dread." This "sad dread" is elaborated two stanzas below in the invocation to night:

> . . . In thy sable mantle us enwrap,
> From feare of perrill and foule horror free.
> Let no false treason seeke us to entrap,
> Nor any dread disquiet once annoy
> The safety of our joy;
> But let the night be calme, and quietsome,
> Without tempestuous storms or sad afray. . .

and again in the following stanza which catalogues more fully the disturbances which night might bring:

> Let no lamenting cryes, nor dolefull teares,
> Be heard all night within, nor yet without:
> Ne let false whispers, breeding hidden feares,
> Breake gentle sleepe with misconceived dout.
> Let no deluding dreames, nor dreadfull sights,
> Make sudden sad affrights. . .

---

[19] H. S. V. Jones, *A Spenser Handbook* (New York, 1930), p. 354.

Here quite clearly the night sounds are not only the effects of nightmares or apparition; they are ambiguous enough to suggest by extension the potential suffering which a lifetime of marriage, not only the wedding night, might involve. The "doleful tears," the "false whispers," /227/ the "misconceived dout," suggest the jealousies and suspicions which conceivably could threaten the marriage and which must be exorcised. Spenser is too tactful to refer to this possibility directly.[20] After making this veiled allusion, he fills out his catalogue with more fanciful fears—of witches, hobgoblins, ghosts, creatures which the town maidens might believe in—and modulates to a lighter tone with the concluding "quire of frogs still croaking." The ominous associations of darkness are evoked again, however, in the last stanza, where the stars are described as torches in the temple of heaven

> that to us wretched earthly clods
> In dreadful darkness lend desired light. . .

Here it is not only the marriage but the whole of human experience which is menaced by the night's sad dread. Thus the threat of disaster, the irrational fear of vaguely specified suffering, hovers faintly over the poem, lending particular urgency to the concluding prayers. It is perhaps not too fanciful to relate the wolves of the fourth stanza to this cluster of night associations and to find in the decorative invocation to the "lightfoot maids" an added symbolic nuance:

> And eke, ye lightfoot mayds, which keepe the deere,
> That on the hoary mountayne used to towre;
> And the wylde wolves, which seeke them to devoure,
> With your steele darts doo chace from comming neer;
> Be also present heere. . .

---

[20] Sidney, who wrote an epithalamion for a fictive, pastoral marriage, did not need to be so tactful. His poem contains a wry catalogue of marital abuses:

> "All churlish words, shrewd answers, crabbed looks,
>   All privateness, self-seeking, inward spite,
>   All waywardness, which nothing kindly brooks,
>   All strife for toys and claiming master's right,
>   Be hence, aye put to flight;
>   All stirring husband's hate
>   'Gainst neighbour's good for womanish debate,
>   Be fled, as things most vain:
>   O Hymen, long their coupled joys maintain!"

Spenser would have known this catalogue, but his own catalogue of night sounds is the closest approach he makes to it.

The imagery of light is even more ubiquitous. References to the sun, as well as to the moon and stars, recur repeatedly. The sun is associated with brightness, with beauty, with joyfulness; it presides over the wakefulness and activity of the day. The sunlit day is the time of social joy, ritualistic joy; the night, if it is moonlit and starlit, if it is atypical in its silent tranquillity, is the time of personal intimate joy. Both day and night have their respective culminations: day at the center of the poem, night at the conclusion. The act of dressing, which is emphasized in the poem, suggests the personal preparation to meet the active, social, /228/ audible world outside the chamber. Placed in this context, the conventional bedding of the bride, which is also described, suggests the retirement from the social context, from sound, from public ritual, from the "delights forepast" of the merchants' daughters.

The accumulation of subtle and unlabored suggestions like these helps to enrich the meaning with which Spenser informs the wedding event. That meaning is in fact very rich. Ultimately the *Epithalamion* is distinguished by its amplitude. It is in every sense a major poem: by its unusual narrative range, embracing *all* the events of the wedding day, by its emotional range, distinguishing with sensitivity and precision related sets of feelings, and by its allusive range, employing without shock a wealth of pagan figures to orchestrate an essentially Christian statement. The world of the poem may be seen as a series of concentric areas. In the center is the couple, always at the dramatic focus; about them lies the town, the "social context"—the merchants' daughters, the young men who ring the bells, the boys who cry "Hymen" with "strong confused noyce"; beyond lies the natural setting, the woods that echo the jubilation with an answering joy, the "cheereful birds," the Mulla, the hoary mountain, and at night the choir of croaking frogs; vaguely outside of this is the world of classical figures, the Muses and the Graces, Maia and Alcmena, Hera, Cynthia, and Hymen, and "Jove's sweet paradice of Day and Night"; finally above all these realms stretches the thinly disguised Christian Heaven, the "temple of the gods," lending light to wretched earthly clods. The poem begins and ends with the widest perspective; at the center of the poem, during the ceremony, the focus has narrowed to the couple itself. Immediately before and after the ceremony the focus includes the "social context." The opening, with its perspective into the past, is balanced by the concluding perspective into the future. Thus, structurally as well as thematically, the amplitude is complemented with an elegant symmetry and an intricate harmony.

If one asks what ideal event is called into being by Spenser's injunctions, the answer is not simple. The event has been social and religious and sexual, and there are hints of a relationship to nature, of a cosmic dimension also. But the richness of Spenser's interpretation is centered in the personal experience of the bridegroom-speaker; the wedding is above all a private emotional event. Because the two roles are fused, the wedding is seen from within, not without. This kind of unconventionality is the most basic of all. Instead of *makarismos*, the assertion of happiness, Spenser achieves the dramatic realization of happiness.

George Puttenham

The Maner of Reioysings at Mariages and Weddings*

As the consolation of children well begotten is great, no lesse but rather greater ought to be that which is occasion of children, that is honorable matrimonie, a loue by al lawes allowed, not mutable nor encombred with such vaine cares & passions, as that other loue, whereof there is no assurance, but loose and fickle affection occasioned for the most part by sodaine sights and acquaintance of no long triall or experience, nor vpon any other good ground wherein any suretie may be conceiued: wherefore the Ciuill Poet could do no lesse in conscience and credit, then as he had before done to the ballade of birth, now with much better deuotion to celebrate by his poeme the chearefull day of mariages aswell Princely as others, for that hath always bene accompted with euery country and nation of neuer so barbarous people the highest & holiest of any ceremonie apperteining to man; a match forsooth made for euer and not for a day, a solace prouided for youth, a comfort for age, a knot of alliance & amitie indissoluble: great reioysing was therefore due to such a matter and to so gladsome a time. This was done in ballade wise, as the natall song, and was song very sweetely by Musitians at the chamber dore of the Bridegroome and Bride at such times as shalbe hereafter declared, and they were called *Epithalamies*, as much to say as ballades at the bedding of the bride: for such as were song at the borde at dinner or supper were other Musickes and not properly *Epithalamies*. Here, if I shall say that which apperteineth to th'arte, and disclose the misterie of the whole matter, I must and doe with all humble reuerence bespeake pardon of the chaste and honorable eares, least I should either offend them with

---

* From George Puttenham, *The Arte of English Poesie*, 1589. Reprinted in *The Arte of English Poesie*, ed. Gladys Willcock and Alice Walker. London: Cambridge University Press, 1936.

licentious speach, or leaue them ignorant of the ancient guise in old times vsed at weddings, in my simple opinion nothing reproueable. This *Epithalamie* was deuided by breaches into three partes to serue for three seuerall fits or times to be song. The first breach was song at the first part of the night, when the spouse and her husband were brought to their bed, & at the very chamber dore, where in a large vtter roome vsed to be (besides the musitiens) good store of ladies or gentlewomen of their kinsefolkes, & others who came to honor the mariage; & the tunes of the songs were very loude and shrill, to the intent there might no noise be hard out of the bed chamber by the skreeking and outcry of the young damosell feeling the first forces of her stiffe & rigorous young man, she being, as all virgins, tender & weake, and vnexpert in those maner of affaires. For which purpose also they vsed by old nurses (appointed to that seruice) to suppresse the noise by casting of pottes full of nuttes round about the chamber vpon the hard floore or pauement, for they vsed no mattes nor rushes as we doe now. So as the Ladies and gentlewomen should haue their eares so occupied what with Musicke, and what with their handes wantonly scambling and catching after the nuttes, that they could not intend to harken after any other thing. This was, as I said, to diminish the noise of the laughing lamenting spouse. The tenour of that part of the song was to congratulate the first acquaintance and meeting of the young couple, allowing of their parents good discretions in making the match, then afterward to sound cherfully to the onset and first encounters of that amorous battaile, to declare the comfort of children, & encrease of loue by that meane cheifly caused: the bride shewing her self euery waies well disposed, and still supplying occasions of new lustes and loue to her husband by her obedience and amorous embracings and all other allurementes. About midnight or one of the clocke, the Musicians came again to the chamber dore (all the Ladies and other women as they were of degree hauing taken their leaue, and being gone to their rest). This part of the ballade was to refresh the faint and weried bodies and spirits, and to animate new appetites with cherefull wordes, encoraging them to the recontinuance of the same entertainments, praising and commending (by supposall) the good conformities of them both, & their desire one to vanquish the other by such frendly conflictes; alledging that the first embracementes neuer bred barnes, by reason of their ouermuch affection and heate, but onely made passage for children and enforced greater liking to the late made match; that the second assaultes were lesse rigorous, but more vigorous and apt to auance the purpose of procreation; that therefore they should persist in all good appetite with an inuincible courage to the end. This was the second part of the

Epithalamie. In the morning when it was faire broad day, & that by liklyhood all tournes were sufficiently serued, the last actes of the enterlude being ended, & that the bride must within few hours arise and apparrell her selfe, no more as a virgine but as a wife, and about dinner time must by order come forth *Sicut sponsa de thalamo* very demurely and stately to be sene and acknowledged of her parents and kinsfolkes whether she were the same woman or a changeling, or dead or aliue, or maimed by any accident nocturnall, the same Musicians came againe with this last part and greeted them both with a Psalme of new applausions, for that they had either of them so well behaued them selues that night, the husband to rob his spouse of her maidenhead and saue her life, the bride so lustely to satisfie her husbandes loue and scape with so litle daunger of her person; for which good chaunce that they should make a louely truce and abstinence of that warre till next night, sealing the placard of that louely league with twentie maner of sweet kisses; then by good admonitions enformed them to the frugall & thriftie life all the rest of their dayes, the good man getting and bringing home, the wife sauing that which her husband should get, therewith to be the better able to keepe good hospitalitie, according to their estates, and to bring vp their children (if God sent any) vertuously, and the better by their owne good example; finally to perseuer all the rest of their life in true and inuiolable wedlocke. This ceremony was omitted when men maried widowes or such as had tasted the frutes of loue before (we call them well experienced young women), in whom there was no feare of daunger to their persons, or of any outcry at all, at the time of those terrible approches. Thus much touching the vsage of *Epithalamie* or bedding ballad of the ancient times, in which if there were any wanton or lasciuious matter more than ordinarie, which they called *F[es]cenina licentia*, it was borne withal for that time because of the matter no lesse requiring. *Catullus* hath made of them one or two very artificiall and ciuil; but none more excellent then of late yeares a young noble man of Germanie, as I take it, *Iohannes secundus*, who, in that and in his poeme *De basiis*, passeth any of the auncient or moderne Poetes in my iudgment.

Philosophy

E. E. Stoll

From Poets & Playwrights: Shakespeare, Jonson, Spenser, Milton, *1930**

Spenser[1]

Spenser is the high priest of English romanticism. Not only was he the leader of the romantic spirit in the Elizabethan Age, but he afterwards presided over what we call the Romantic Revival. Shakespeare and Milton were the names then held most in reverence, but the spirit abroad was Spenser's. Without him, of course, there would have been a revival, but one wonders if it would have been quite the same. All the leaders and chief personalities felt in some way his impress, came at some time under his spell,—Thomson and Shenstone, the Wartons and Chatterton, Gray and Collins, Wordsworth and Coleridge, Byron and Shelley; and towards the end of the period his presence towered still higher, and benignly overshadowed Leigh Hunt and Keats. The poets' poet Lamb called him, Hazlitt said he was of all poets the most poetical, and perhaps no English singer has taught so many. The chief critics, also, of the romantic age analyzed his qualities and celebrated his merits—not only Lamb, Hazlitt, and Hunt, but the Wartons and Coleridge.

1

What is romanticism, what do we mean by this over-used, ill-used word? Primarily we mean what has to do with chivalry, a life devoted to love and glory, with ad- /168/ ventures and tourneys, and the showy

---

* From E. E. Stoll, *Poets & Playwrights: Shakespeare, Jonson, Spenser, Milton.* Minneapolis: University of Minnesota Press, 1930, pp. 167–179. Reprinted by permission of the publisher and the author.

[1] In part this essay was delivered as a public lecture at Vassar in January, 1927. I have not undertaken to remove certain direct and intimate touches, and *argumenta ad feminam*, which were suggested by the occasion.

fairy-tale life of knights and ladies. That we find in Spenser. Sometimes we mean what has to do with romance (a kindred word, with a kindred meaning), a life high-uplifted above the practical and humdrum, and devoted to a dreamy or rapturous love, even though no knights and ladies may be there. And that we find in Spenser. Sometimes we mean the subtle and mysterious aspects of the poetic imagination, whereby more is meant than meets the ear, as in Wordsworth's or Shelley's poetry of nature, or in the supernatural or legendary as touched to new life by Coleridge in the *Ancient Mariner* and *Christabel*, or by Keats in *La Belle Dame Sans Merci*. And that we find in Spenser too, though it is, of course, not quite like theirs,—how like and how different I hope before the end to show.

Now behind all these meanings—the more literal, the more spiritual, and that which is rather esthetic—there lurks a background of the medieval. The Romantic Revival was a medieval revival; and the spirit of romance was born not in the Middle Ages, indeed, but under their influence. Yet Spenser is not medieval but of the Renaissance; and the Renaissance, as we ordinarily think of it, turned its back on the Middle Ages and faced the world, directly or in the mirror of ancient art.

2

What then is the Renaissance? You may sometime have seen Leonardo da Vinci's St. John the Baptist. He is a beautiful young man, bowing before the little Saviour with a bewitching smile, with a cross in his hand and some raiment of camel's hair about him, but looking as if he had fed not on locusts at all but only on the wild honey. Or, on the other hand, you may have seen Botticelli's Venus, newly arisen out of the sea, the goddess of love /169/ and laughter, but here with the wistful look in her face of Botticelli's Madonnas, a goddess (the ancients had none) of sorrow and tears. Here, and there, is the Renaissance—the Middle Ages discovering and entering into the classical world, Christianity and paganism, holiness and happiness, meeting and mingled, and the spirit reluctantly or unreluctantly reunited with the flesh.

To be more explicit, the Renaissance also (as the word of course signifies) is a revival,—of learning, of the arts, above all of interest and delight in the world as a whole. The Middle Ages lay under the shadow of the Church, and though men there often contrived to take their pleasure it was not with the best of consciences. And they were ignorant, hardly knowing how to take it; the treasures of antiquity were as yet closed to them, and the arts they practiced were traditional and simple. Some of the fine art was very noble—for instance, the poetry of Dante and Chaucer, the architecture of France, the painting of Italy. But medieval literature, even the best of it in some measure, and the less good in greater measure, suffered for the lack of certain qualities now to be introduced through an acquaintance with the classics. The ancients were distinguished by an appreciation of the principle of beauty and harmony. In ethics and conduct they looked to the ideal of balance, of the golden mean; in art they did the same. In the best period they did not despise the senses; neither did they worship them. They loved life but they loved their ideals too. They were neither ascetics on the one hand nor debauchees on the other. In the Middle Ages men were. But now it was a new and freer life that men were entering, the old having gone stale; it was a new and freer art that men were beginning to practice, the old having become almost meaningless.

In their delight in the new, the whole-hearted children /170/ of the Renaissance, like Ariosto, Spenser's master, even turned, as Spenser did not, ironically and cynically against the old. In the *Orlando Furioso* Ariosto was a poet of chivalry before him, but half in sport. The high-flown sentiments and extravagant adventures are there, and all is very gay and gallant, but his knights and ladies are at heart almost satyrs and nymphs, courtiers and courtesans; and their romance is but skin-deep. His knights are to Spenser's somewhat as are the gallants of Charles II's time to Sidney and Raleigh. And in part, though, as we shall see, not wholly, the difference between the two poets is owing to the English temper as compared with the Italian, to Spenser's character as compared with Ariosto's, and to the fact that though the latter comes more than two generations earlier than the former he belongs to the late Renaissance, Spenser to the early. For in that movement England was more than a century behind.

3

Spenser looks back reverently to the Middle Ages but is certainly of the Renaissance. Still young in heart, with the bloom on his soul, and his pure romantic dream untroubled, he entered into the new world and the spirit of classical poetry. And he did it with a sprightly and delicate delight. He knew the classics as no English poet had known them before him; and in his verse he was closer than any had ever been to their spirit. He had a finer taste than his predecessors and many of his successors. He knew the Greeks, whereas even many of his contemporary Elizabethans know them only in Latin; and he knew some of the Greek tragic poets, who to Shakespeare and his fellows seem in any form to have been strangers. He seems to have preferred Virgil to Ovid, as few Elizabethans, including Shakespeare, had learned to do; and /171/ Plato and the Platonic doctrines were his particular joy and enthusiasm. Indeed, Spenser is the one great poet of the early Elizabethan Age to drink deep of the cup of classical literature and also feel the new life tingling in his veins.

The two then went well together, though they do not today. For us the reading of classical literature does not any longer mean the discovery of life itself. It meant that to Italian painters like Botticelli and Leonardo, as well as to the poets of Europe. It opened men's eyes, freed them for their medieval fears and superstitions, revealed reality and its beauty. For instance, men now began to draw, paint, sculpture, or poetically describe the nude—a thing which men had not done for a thousand years. The fact may be taken as typical. Men were discovering the very world, the world about them—the thrill of that discovery is the Renaissance—and what is the discovery of the moons of Jupiter, or of the American Continent, to that?

But Spenser was not a classicist, any more than he was a realist, though he came in contact with reality. Few in the Renaissance were. Few then were so classical as Milton was to be. And the special and peculiar charm of the early Renaissance is the medieval spirit in a classical garb. Or without a garb, perhaps we should say. Botticelli's Venus with the soul and face of a Madonna, stands there like the Greek goddess that she is, unclad. Just so Spenser blends elements strangely incongruous—Christian and pagan history, Christian and pagan mythology, saints and satyrs. In the *Fairy Queen*, the lady Una, who represents the Church, lives for a time with the satyrs, at her ease. Even at school you read Browning's *The Bishop Orders his Tomb in St. Praxed's*. There is the Renaissance, though the late Renaissance, materialistic and corrupt as /172/ Spenser was not, but not yet cynical or mocking. It is thus the dying Bishop's tomb is to be sculptured, if his sons will heed him in his pleading: Give me, he says,

> Those Pans and Nymphs ye wot of, and perchance
> Some tripod, thyrsus, with a vase or so,
> The Saviour at his sermon on the mount,
> St. Praxed in a glory, and one Pan
> Ready to twitch the Nymph's last garment off,—
> And Moses with the tables—

There's a mixture for you, from a bishop's deathbed at that! So the tomb in which Luini, Leonardo's contemporary, in the picture now at the Brera, has the angels place the corpse of Saint Catherine, is sculptured over with Tritons and Nereids.

And much in Spenser is, whether consciously or unconsciously, deliberately or inadvertently, old-fashioned and medieval enough. There is almost no allegory in the classics, and Spenser abounds in allegory.

And, besides, the *Fairy Queen* is a tale of chivalry, and the vocabulary is intentionally archaic. Chivalry and feudalism are dead and gone, and quite properly Spenser puts a medieval flavor into his language as he treats of them. Really, he is like Sir Walter Scott in his poems and novels, Coleridge in the *Ancient Mariner,* or the preraphaelite Morris and Rossetti, as he turns from the present to the past. He takes to the poetic beauty of a period now gone by. But though he returns to it, like them he is not of it; there's the blue haze of distance upon it, or the ivy and the mellow patina of time. It is romantic not much more because it is of chivalry than because it is unreal and remote. Like the Romantic poets and the Preraphaelites, he relishes old words like *eftsoones* and *whilom, wight* for *man* or *person, eke* for *also,* and *paynim* for *pagan.* Like Scott, from afar, he delights in battle and all the paraphernalia and /173/ bravery of battle. "Fair shields, gay steeds, bright arms be my delight," cries his Sir Guyon. And like Keats he dreams of the loves of knights and ladies, their courtesy and gallantry. To him these things were still more picturesque and precious than to Chaucer simply because he had read of them rather than seen them—read of them in Chaucer himself, in romances like *Sir Gawain and the Green Knight,* or in Malory. He does not invoke the muse, it is worth noting, in the regular style of Homer, Virgil, and Milton, and beseech her to sing, but prays her to vouchsafe to him the yellow rolls of manuscript. "Lay forth out of thine everlasting scryne, The antique rolles which there lye hidden still, Of Faerie knights and fairest Tanaquill." Chatterton, Scott, or Keats might have said the same.

Indeed, despite superficial appearances, and the difference between him and Ariosto, Spenser's deepest debt, perhaps, was to the classics and the Italians and to the new spirit in the world about him. What made him romantic was not the medieval life which he knew of but his attitude toward it, the glamour of the past, the esthetic delight of the poet himself. There is, as Professor Mackail has noticed, a romantic spirit in Theocritus and also in Virgil, though with no age of knighthood behind them; they too look to the past with a tender regret; and while this attitude of theirs as such may never have affected Spenser at all, the exquisiteness of the ancients and the Italians did. And exquisiteness, a delight in beauty and in emotions somewhat for their own sake, and a regard for detail, are, as later we shall see more clearly, at the bottom of the romantic spirit. Before, then, we attempt to define Spenser's romanticism and to distinguish it from Milton's and our own, it is well to consider Spenser's indebtedness further, and not only the nature /174/ of his art in general but those qualities of it which are not specifically or necessarily romantic at all.

4

To the ancients and the Italians Spenser and others like him in the Renaissance must have owed something of their extraordinary exquisiteness and refinement, their delight in emotions and the expression of them for their own sake, since these were little known in England before that day. Such things are slow in developing of themselves, and come, like Theocritus and Virgil, towards the end of a poetic movement. The Italianate English poets ripened quickly, profiting by these high examples. And there is something precocious and premature, mellow and overripe about Sidney and Spenser, as not about Shakespeare, who was comparatively untouched. In them the love of beauty and splendor, like that of fame, characteristic of the Renaissance, is a more all-engrossing passion. Spenser feels them both, and both were either inspired or fostered in him by classical literature. He was profoundly affected, as I have said, by the doctrine of love and beauty in Plato; but he delighted in physical beauty as well as the ideal, inspired by classical and Italian literature again. Love of beauty (with hatred of ugliness, its counterpart) is the motive which animates his poem. Love of beauty, of course, needs no instilling or fostering, but taste and exquisiteness do. The *Fairy Queen* is an allegorical moral poem, but it is a Palace of Pleasure, a Paradise of Dainty Devices. It is a treasure-house of lovely descriptions of lovely things—processions and pageants, garments and trappings, landscapes and gardens, trees and flowers, birds and animals, but, above all, women and girls. Spenser is like Benozzo Gozzoli in the Campo Santo at Pisa and the Riccardi Palace at Florence, delighting in palaces /175/ and processions, birds and beasts, and like the Venetians, reveling in the glory of the nude. And that the delight in the beauty of these things may be perfect and complete, they are all spirited away into the past, to a land of dreams.

5

His delight in the physical beauty of women is exquisite but eager, sensuous but sane. Classical and Italian influence had opened his eyes to the beauty of the body, and had given him the courage, and shown him the way, to express it. Few things in the *Fairy Queen* are so delightful as the figures of ladies, maidens, and nymphs that go glancing through its changing vistas. Nowere is the play of his fancy happier, or the cadence of his verse tenderer, than here. I well remember as a boy my delight at coming upon this description of Belphœbe:

> Upon her eyelids many graces sate,
> Under the shadow of her even browes.

Epithalamion

Such a gracious shadow there is under the brows of the Praxitelean Aphrodites, which Spenser never saw; both he and Praxiteles saw it where we all may see it today for ourselves. "The beauty of women," as Mr. de Selincourt observes, "again and again suggests to him imaginative effects of light and shade." The damsels who dance, before the knight in Acrasia's Bower—

> every of them strove, with most delights,
> Him to aggrate, and greatest pleasures shew;
> Some framd faire lookes, glancing like evening lights,
> Others sweet words, dropping like honny dew.

They "used their eyes," as women will. And the eyes, lips, and hair of women play a great part in Spenser, as in Dante, but more richly and sensuously, as in our Preraphaelites or in the fancy and memory of any lover. /176/ Britomart, again, the disguised maiden warrior, when she unlaces her helmet, and lets her golden hair fall down to her heels, springing a surprise upon the natives, a *coup de théâtre*, reminds him of the northern lights:

> Like as the shining skie in summers night,
> What time the dayes with scorching heat abound,
> Is creasted all with lines of firie light,
> That it prodigious seemes in common peoples sight.

And even of Acrasia, the queen of voluptuous pleasure, he says, that

> her faire eyes, sweet smyling in delight,
> Moystened their firie beames, with which she thrild
> Fraile hearts, yet quenched not; like starry light
> Which, sparkling on the silent waves, does seeme more bright.

With which she thrild fraile hearts yet quenched not—the sentiment and style (before the time) of *Epipsychidion*; and that figure to picture the eye of a woman in love George Meredith does not disdain to use in the great farewell scene of *Richard Feverel*. And all three figures— this one, that of the evening lights, and that of the Aurora— show how sensitively his imagination responded to the most intangible and ethereal beauty, natural or human, that there is in the world.

Such exquisiteness and audacity of expression seem classical or Italian; the tenderness and deep spirit of chivalry seem rather English, though the racial line cannot be clearly drawn. It is all of the Renaissance, and is as romantic as heart could desire. The spirit of chivalry, indeed, is medieval, for he follows the example of the old romances, and presents every knight as the servant of a lady, and the chief source of virtue in the poem as woman's love; but the Renaissance had refined upon the idea, Spenser joining with it. If the love of money is the root of all evil, the love of woman, Spenser and Sidney to- /177/ gether would have said, is the root of all bliss; and the *Fairy Queen*, though a code of conduct, is a book of gallantry throughout. For the poet the path of virtue is the service of the fair; and even the pursuit of wisdom is not more arduous. His hero is taught by some allegorical character, and this is oftenest a fair woman, who takes him aside, with his hand in hers. Instruction in Spenser, and in medieval allegory generally, is as it used to be (and probably still is) in the Sunday School—males are not taught by males. Spenser himself must have been as fine a gentleman as ever lived. Greater geniuses like Chaucer and Shakespeare are sometimes coarse and low, but Spenser, though for the purposes of allegory sometimes coarse, is never low. No one is sweeter or more tender. He was the friend of the first gentlemen of the day, Sidney and Raleigh, and the purpose of his poem as he described it in his letter to Raleigh was to fashion a gentleman or noble person in virtuous and gentle discipline. And according to Spenser as well as the courtesybooks of the time the source of virture was love—love for friend or woman. Gentlemen then frequented the court, and as Spenser himself says of the court of Elizabeth,

> love most aboundeth there,
> For all the walls and windows there are writ
> All full of love, and love, and love, my deare,
> And all their talk and studee is of it.

That is, the windows were inscribed with love-sonnets, cut with the lover's own diamond, as is the glass, I notice, in the windows of some college fraternities. Is that all of the old-time court life that lives on in college? At court the study of love and the study of virtue were one— no wonder we call those the good old times.

Even at college, however, the court of Elizabeth would /178/ seem today to be a little absurd. As at that of Urbino, where dwelt Castiglione, author of the great book of courtesy, every courtier was not only a lover but must needs be in love with the lady on the throne. Thus love of woman becomes love of country; and in the *Fairy Queen* it is well-nigh life itself. Not only is almost every man and woman, good or bad, a lover; but he lives to love or to fight, and fights even for love. How romantic—all love and sport, all play and no work, as at college again! But for that matter it is almost so in Shakespeare, and Shakespeare is not tiresome or silly. As in Shakespeare, all high-born women

Epithalamion 67

in the *Fairy Queeen* are beautiful, just as all high-born men can ride,[2] fight, and make love—it is a romantic world. And as in Shakespeare, though more than in him, but not more than in Dante, love conquers all, and even when in error, lovers are liberally indulged. Dante is almost swept away from his moral moorings by his own tale of Francesca; and Spenser, while Sir Guyon is destroying Acrasia's Bower, makes her and her maidens touch him so nearly that the reader wonders how he can bring himself to do it.

> And in amours the passing hours to spend!

The sweetness of the verse betrays him—Spenser would have liked so to spend them himself. Chastity is represented by Britomart, a lady, armed like Athena, but cherishing a passion.

> A harder lesson, to learne Continence
> In joyous pleasure than in grievous paine,

says the poet, contradicting Aristotle, in the true spirit of romance. And the one lesson in the House of Holiness /179/ that the Red-Cross Knight finds "too too hard for living clay" is to abandon his romantic career:

> But deeds of arms must I at last be faine,
> And ladies love to leave, so dearly bought?

But it is not required of him.

Yet Spenser was not infatuated or obsessed. Like most romantic persons, he was conservative; and like most romantic men, he wanted a woman to be ladylike rather than womanly,—Una and Britomart when they are not quite ladylike are only the *more* romantic,—even as romantic women want a man to be gentlemanly rather than manly. He believed in what in America is no longer believed in and what perhaps you, in these latter days, have never even heard of—women keeping to their sphere. Those who don't keep to it he puts in hell, to recompense them for the hell they have made of heaven:

> Amongst these mighty men were wemen mixed,
> Proud wemen, vaine, forgetfull of their yoke:
> The bold Semiramis . . .

---

[2] As feates of armes, and love to entertaine,
But chiefly skill to ride, seems a science
Proper to gentle bloud.—II, iv, 1.

but the catalogue I spare you. And some of his heroes are shrewdly aware of women's wiles,—

> And all the wyles of wemen's wits know passing well,—

though one has a rather naïve way of warding them off:

> But he was wise and wary of her will,
> And ever held his hand upon his hart.

Concealing, he reveals. He is simpler than a farmer at a fair, with his hand clutched in his pocket. But against their wiles what but simplicity ever availed? He is not a farmer.

Virgil K. Whitaker

From The Religious Basis of Spenser's Thought, *1950**

In short, although Spenser may have shared a very few of the Puritans' distinctive notions, such as their dislike of the "lordship" of bishops, he was a Puritan only in the sense that every man is who hates corruption and incompetence. So was Chaucer when he wrote of his Parson, who stands in marked contrast to his other ecclesiastics:

> To drawen folk to hevene by fairnesse,
> By good ensample, this was his bisynesse . . . .
> But Cristes loore and his apostles twelve
> He taught, but first he folwed it hymselve. (*Prologue*, ll. 519–28)

So was Sir Thomas More when he wrote slyly at the beginning of his discussion of religion in Utopia: "They have priests of exceeding holiness, and therefore very few." But Spenser was certainly not a member of the Elizabethan Puritan party, at least in so far as they were attacking episcopacy and the Established Church; nor did he sympathize with them. Quite the contrary. In the *Shepheardes Calender* he spoke for a body of men who were trying to establish Anglicanism soundly and to defend it in the most effective way possible—by purifying and strengthening it—and to preserve as much as possible of its Catholic heritage. The *Calender* is a unique poetic expression of the ideals of the ablest and sincerest adherents of the Elizabethan Settlement; and it is also a unique historical document, as the very misunderstanding of it testifies, for it shows us the interests and ideals of a group whose very existence at so early a date has often gone unrecognized. . . . /68/

---

* From Virgil K. Whitaker, *The Religious Basis of Spenser's Thought*. Stanford: Stanford University Press, 1950, pp. 23, 68–70. Reprinted by permission of the publisher and the author.

Recent scholarship has thoroughly established Spenser as no mere writer of beautiful verses but as a sincere and careful ethical thinker, fusing artistic skill and study and thought into a wonderful poetic whole. He must also be recognized as a careful theological and religious thinker with a position of his own. Once the initial assumption that he was a Puritan is abandoned, that position becomes simple and reasonably consistent, nor is there any fundamental change in outlook from his earliest to his latest work. The growing interest in Platonism that is apparent in his later poems perhaps led him to accentuate the Platonic element that had always been a part of Christian mysticism and to add concepts from Renaissance neo-Platonism, so that the treatment of the journey of the mind to God in the *Hymnes of Heavenly Love* and *Heavenly Beautie* is Platonic, whereas in the House of Holiness it is predominantly ecclesiastical. But even that shift of emphasis involved no change in doctrine or party loyalty.

Spenser's position can perhaps be described somewhat as follows: He demands a church that shall be honest and efficient in its corporate life, true, in the main, to the tenets of the Reformation, but retaining much of the ceremonial and the spiritual life of the past. He has little sympathy for radical new ideas or, for that matter, for controversy—the books and papers that are the vomit of error (I, i, 20).

For Roman Catholicism as a political force Spenser has the intense hatred of a patriotic Englishman. Duessa is outfitted with mitre and gold (I, ii, 13), and Orgoglio gives her the triple tiara of the Papacy and the seven-headed /69/ beast of Revelations (I, vii, 16–17). He also hates the Inquisition (cf. I, viii, 36; V, xi, 19). But Duessa seems totally uninterested in Roman Catholic doctrines or ceremonies; and, except for such details as holy water, images, paxes, and Aves and Pater Nosters that hide ignorance, Spenser does not specifically attack them.

For the Puritans Spenser has little sympathy except in so far as their demand for an honest and educated clergy agrees with his. The Blatant Beast is undoubtedly a satire upon their quarreling and scandalmongering, as well as upon their iconoclasm (VI, xii, 22–25). So is Spenser's scathing allusion to "that vngracious crew which faines demurest grace" (VII, vii, 35).[179] Perhaps Sans Joy also glances in their direction, especially in that his next youngest brother is Sans Loy, just as Puritanism was followed by anarchy in church and state. Spenser had perhaps read Calvin, and there may be traces of his influence. But Spenser is no Calvinist. When he agrees with Calvin, Calvin in turn agrees with general Protestant or even general Christian thought. Where Spenser

---

[179] Cf. Padelford, *Political and Ecclesiastical Allegory*, p. 10.

reveals his stand on crucial issues between Anglicanism and Calvinism, he invariably disagrees with Calvin.

Perhaps, finally, it is not too ingenious to see in the episodes of Book I, Cantos iv and v, a summary of Spenser's position. Red Cross has been guided by Duessa, disguised as Fidessa, to the House of Pride and has witnessed its hollow display. He is then challenged by Sans Joy and almost beaten, when "quickening faith, that earst was woxen weak," revives him. Is Spenser trying to say that Red Cross, bereft of Una or religious truth, vacillates between Rome and Puritanism and that his natural reaction to an exhibit of pride is extreme Puritanism, until he is saved by a revival of faith? Perhaps this is too fanciful. But at least Spenser emerges as the religious fellow of Hooker[180] and ancestor of Herbert, as he is the poetical /70/ fellow of Sidney and ancestor of Milton. He is also a leader in the very front rank of a major intellectual and religious movement of his age; and, as such, he grows in intellectual stature, whether or not one approves of the direction in which he is moving. He is, finally, the first literary representative of the *via media*—and, it might be added, of the vulnerability to misinterpretation that has always been associated with the middle way!

---

[180] The following remarks by Davis (*Edmund Spenser*, pp. 242–43), which seem to the writer an excellent summary of one aspect of Spenser's thought, reveal his intellectual kinship with Hooker. They are especially interesting in that they rest on an assumption that Spenser was at some time and in some respects a Puritan: "For the whole universe, 'in part, and eeke in generall,' is ruled not by unseen chance but by visible 'law of kind'—this is the substance of Nature's retort to Mutability, the personification of all the grosser and undisciplined elements in cosmic and physical creation.

"To aid the working of universal law is the high prerogative of man. Endowed with reason and free-will he is master of his fate, cleaving his way towards the highest good. If he fail, the fault is not in his stars nor in divine predestination, but in himself. If he succeed, virtue proves its own reward.... So Nature enjoins no blind acceptance of theological dogma nor the sacrifice of present reality to an unknown future, but a sense of responsibility, conformity with the law of self-development whereby every creature, fulfilling its destiny, may further the realisation of divine purpose."

W. L. Renwick

From Daphnäida and Other Poems, *1929**

Fowre Hymnes

As our business is with Spenser's poems and not with the history of philosophy, it is unnecessary to discuss the spread of Platonism in Renaissance Europe. Spenser would meet it at Cambridge and find it fashionable in writing and discussion, and, himself amorous by nature and keenly alive to beauty, would certainly find it attractive, for of all Plato's work the part which was most canvassed was his spiritualising of love and beauty, his raising of them to a philosophical dignity which mediæval philosophy, dominated by ascetic theology, could not allow. The works of Plato were available to him with the useful Latin version of Ficino, and he was certainly acquainted with the classics of Renaissance Platonism, Ficino's commentary on the *Symposium,* Benevieni's *Canzone d'Amore* with the commentary of Pico della Mirandola, Bembo's *Asolani,* the third Book of Castiglione's *Corteggiano* translated by Hoby. There are other treatises which he may have known, such as Leone Hebreo's *Dialoghi di Amore,* Sperone's Dialogue, Bruno's *Degli Heroici Furori,* Loys le Roy's commentary on the *Symposium,* and so on, not to mention what he would find in his Cicero. The difficulty of "sources" here, indeed, is like that of the *Amoretti,* that much of the matter is common to several authors all of whom Spenser probably knew. In illustrating these poems, therefore, I have adopted somewhat the same method, and have cited for preference the treatise of Ficino, the primary authority, and the *Courtier* of Castiglione in Hoby's translation, the most readily available to Spenser, which is also the most suc-

---

* From W. L. Renwick (ed.), *Daphnäida and Other Poems.* London: The Scholartis Press, 1929, pp. 209–213. Reprinted by permission of the publisher and the author.

cinct, the least entangled with speculations foreign to Spenser, and, in short, the best representative of the common conception of Platonism circulating among those who were not professed philosophers. It will be understood that these notes are illustrative and not exhaustive.

This treatment is the more necessary as Spenser's use of his Platonic treatises is uneven and uncertain. We must not think of him as sitting with his books open before him, rendering this Latin paragraph and that Italian sentence into English verse and fitting the whole /210/ laboriously together to make a systematic thesis. He had his own ends to serve, and with all his pleasure in his authorities, and all his indebtedness to them, it is quite another matter to what extent he subscribed to their doctrine. We must, first of all, observe his own warning and take the two pairs of poems separately. In the first two Hymnes he writes as a lover, and selects from his Platonists the psychological elements which are more or less universal experiences, leaving aside the speculative elements entirely. In the second pair he writes as a Christian, and intertwines—rather than fuses—such of the speculative elements as suit the teaching of the Church and his purposes of the moment.

Let us remind ourselves of the essentials of the doctrine: the contrast of earthly or physical love with heavenly or intellectual: and the "ladder" by which the lover of beauty ascends from one to the other. First of all he contemplates and loves one present beauty in the flesh; then the mental image of that beauty in its absence; then that image without reference to or in preference to its origin in flesh; then, generalising it and combining it with all other images of beauty to make a common beauty contemplated in the mind, which beauty has no definite physical reference but is an end in itself. Thus the mind, turned inward to contemplate this ideal or metaphysical Beauty, gains touch with universal Beauty, which is an aspect of Divinity, and the love of this Universal and Intellectual Beauty is Heavenly Love. In Ficino and Pico this comparatively simple doctine is much involved in mystical mythology, and astrology, and theories of the threefold nature of things, the physical, the intellectual, and the angelic, but—a point to keep in mind—Spenser leaves all that aside.

In the first two Hymnes Spenser ascends the "Platonic ladder" as far as the first stage after the natural love of individual beauty in the flesh—so far, that is, as to enjoy the contemplation of his mistress's beauty in her absence. But he goes no further than the individual. The crucial lines are in the *Hymne of Love*, 192–223, in the *Hymne of Beauty*, 211 to the end. In the first of these passages he rearranges the commonplaces, putting the lover's exploits performed to win his lady's favour after the formation of the mental image of her beauty instead of before it; in the second he definitely recants.

> He thereon (on the image) fixeth all his fantasie, /211/
> And fully setteth his felicitie,
> Counting it fairer, then it is indeed...

In this he echoes Castiglione: "Through the vertue of imagination he shall facion within himself that beawty muche more faire, then it is in deede." But Castiglione's M. Peter Bembo goes on: "And thus (by generalising beauty) he shall beehoulde no more the particular beawtie of one woman, but an universall, that decketh all bodies. Whereupon... he shall litle esteame it, that he sett great store by at the first." And Spenser continues by a recital of the joys of lovers, and a prayer to Venus to soften his lady's heart. The recantation may be read again in *Amoretti* lxxii. As for the contrast of earthly and heavenly love, Spenser does draw a contrast, but it is not a Platonic contrast, for here he trenches on ground wherein the Barbarian is conspicuously superior to the Greek. His contrast is not between human love and the mystical love of Intellectual Beauty, but between two forms of human passion, the real love that is honourable and faithful, and the unreal lust that is faithless and degrading. This is the teaching of Books III and IV of *The Faerie Queene*, and of most decent people; it entered the minds of some of the Platonists, and confused them a little, but for them it is, not being Platonic, a very minor issue. The Platonism of these two Hymnes is, then, elementary and partial. Their end is not the mystical ravishment of the earth-delivered soul in the intellectual contemplation of Divine Beauty, but prayers to Cupid and Venus for aid in the conquest of his obdurate mistress, Rosalind or Elizabeth Boyle or some other. And be it noted that Spenser stopped there, for the other Hymnes, as he tells us himself, were written much later. These are love-poems, in which Spenser used Plato and the Platonists as in other poems he used Virgil and Ariosto and Petrarch. He caught Platonism as he caught the Pastoral and the Sonnet—a convention of thought like the convention of setting and the convention of sentiment—and "imitated" this dignified and fashionable material that had come over with the rest from that almost fabulous Italy.

Though the "influence" was almost wholly literary, helping the poet to recognise and express his own feelings, the implication as well as the prestige of his originals was philosophical, and Spenser confesses his absorption in the physical love of fleshly beauty by writing of Heavenly /212/ Love and Heavenly Beauty. In the *Hymne of Heavenly Love*, however, he does not continue the Platonic ascent, but breaks away to set down the central tenets of Christianity. Here again he preaches doctrine that was to the Greeks foolishness. For though he borrows from his Platonic treatises—and again for purely literary reasons, since he was constructing a parallel to a poem which he had made largely out of them—his subject is the life and death of Christ, his process is one of parallelism rather than of ascent, and his end is Love as taught by St. John and the Christian Churches.

With the fourth Hymne we have to make a fresh start, and that itself betrays a difficulty. For literary reasons Spenser was trying to follow out the movement of the Hymnes of Love and Beauty. In the Platonic scheme the process is simple and logical: beauty is the cause of love. Heavenly Love is the reaction of the soul to Heavenly Beauty, which is indeed proved to exist by the mystical experience which is termed Heavenly Love. But in the *Hymne of Heavenly Love* Spenser was treating of a conception of Love which was quite outwith the Platonic process, in it he had reached his climax, the highest of his faith, and yet his literary parallel demanded a fourth Hymne which by no logical process could follow from his third. Returning then to his Platonists, and remembering his Bible, he began again. Having given over the notion that Heavenly Love is an extension of Earthly, he gave up the idea whose beginning is expressed by Castiglione thus: "Therfore the soule rid of vices, purged with the studies of true Philosophie, occupied in spirituall, and exercised in matters of understandinge, tourning her to the beehoulding in her owne substance . . . seeth in herself a shining beame of that lyght, which is the true image of the aungelic beawtye...." Heavenly Love, according to the third Hymne, is not turned inward, but outward, and Heavenly Beauty is not found within, but is imagined as but immeasurably greater than the beauty of earth: the method of the preacher, not of the philosopher, however much indebted to the Platonists for its phrasing. Spenser had to find a parallel to or substitute for Venus capable of support by Christian authority. In Ficino he found Heavenly Beauty identified with Sapience, and he found Sapience in his Bible and Apocrypha. Difficulty and confusion are evident throughout the poem, and the final vision of Sapience, captured /213/ at one bound without philosophic process, while it may be a real experience as it is not an uncommon experience, is isolated and in so far suspect. There is no hint of it in Spenser's other poems. This is, of course, probably the latest poem of Spenser's we have, and it may be that his mind was turning more to speculation and away from the practical issues to which it had hitherto been confined. On the evidence we have, we can only say that it is strange to his habit as we know it.

Does this mean, then, that Platonism had no influence on Spenser's mind? Certainly his Platonism, as expounded here, is imperfect and alloyed, and its influence has been much exaggerated, but one doctrine remains constant in his thought, the belief in the divine nature of beauty. He did not ascend the "Platonic ladder" from earthly to heavenly beauty; the earth that its Creator found good sufficed for him; but he saw that the Creator had made it beautiful, that its beauty came from Him, and was the mark of its divine origin. Spenser can never be claimed as a deep or even a clear speculative thinker: but perhaps he got the best out of the "Platonism" he knew.

John Smith Harrison

From Platonism in English Poetry of the Sixteenth and Seventeenth Centuries, *1915**

The exposition of the true inward beauty of woman is found in the "Epithalamion" . . . In the account of the dialectic, by which the lover gains a sight of absolute beauty, Plato has stated that at one stage the lover will see that beauty of mind surpasses beauty of outward form. Plato says, "In the next stage he will consider that the beauty of the mind is more honourable than the beauty of outward form." ("Symposium," 210.) This idea lies at the basis of Spenser's praise of beauty in the "Epithalamion." In his marriage hymn he /32/ dwells in exuberant Renaissance fashion upon the physical perfections of the bride, each detail an object of delight to the senses. The sight of such beauty amazes the beholders. But after this is done, Spenser draws attention to the truth that, although these perfections that are visible to the eye may daze the mind, there is a higher beauty of soul which no eye can see. His admiration for the bride's beauty is then caught up into a more lofty pitch and blended with his love of her moral qualities.

---

* From John Smith Harrison, *Platonism in English Poetry of the Sixteenth and Seventeenth Centuries*. New York: Columbia University Press, 1915, pp. 31–32. Reprinted by permission of the publisher and the author.

Imagery and Symbolism

Israel Baroway

The Imagery of Spenser and the *Song of Songs*, 1934*

Though Ponsonbie's preface to Spenser's *Complaints* may be disingenuous on some counts,[1] its ascription of a *"Canticum canticorum* translated" to Spenser is unquestionably reliable.[2] The dispersion and purloining of this work (among the "smale Poemes") "since his departure ouer Sea"[3] may well be part of Ponsonbie's press-agentry,[4] but the fact of its existence certainly is not. In a period when metrical renditions of parts of Scripture, and especially those parts ascribed to Spenser—"The seuen Psalmes," *Ecclesiastes* and the *Song of Songs*— virtually gushed from the pens of England's poets,[5] it were strange indeed to find "the poet's poet" untouched by the aesthetic compulsion which moved Wyatt, Surrey, Gascoigne, Sidney, Chapman, and other poets of the age to shape the mystifying rhythms and the exotic imagery of biblical poetry into familiar Renaissance patterns. A long critical tradition, rooted in patristic exegesis, had firmly established the poetic integrity of the *Song of Songs, even* on the ground of verse;[6]

---

* From *The Journal of English and Germanic Philology*, XXXIII (1934), 23–45. Reprinted by permission of the editors and the author.

[1] *Complaints*, Renwick, ed. (London, 1923), pp. 179–187.

[2] Smith and De Selincourt, eds. *The Poetical Works of Edmund Spenser* (Oxford, 1912), p. 470. Unless otherwise indicated all Spenser references are to this edition.

[3] *Ibid.*

[4] *Complaints, op. cit.*, pp. 179–187.

[5] Thomas Warton, *History of English Poetry from the Close of the 11 Century to the Commencement of the 18 Century* (London, 1840, 3 vols.), III, *passim*.

[6] Criticism as early as Googe held that the "Songs and Ballades of Salomon" "were garnished and set forth with sweet according tunes and heauenly soundes of pleasaunt metre," Warton, *op. cit.*, III, 364–365; Lodge believed that "Salomon voutsafed poetical practices," his verse being "Hexameter and pentameter" (*Elizabethan Critical Essays*, ed. G. G. Smith, I, 71) ; Harington wrote that the Songs of "Salomon" were affirmed by "the learnedest diuines" "to be verse," and "in meetre, though the rule of the Hebrewe verse they agree not on" (*Ibid.*, II, 207) ; the *Arte*

the practice of Spenser's predecessors /24/ and contemporaries had sanctioned the use of biblical material for the exercise of artistic ingenuity. Must we believe that one of the exquisitely sensitive souls of the age and one of its most daring literary adventurers should have reacted less powerfully to the aesthetic values of Holy Writ than did Sandys, or Fraunce, or Stanyhurst, or Herbert, Donne, Vaughan, Crashaw, Quarles, Bacon, Wither, and the remaining host who experimented in verse with the poetry of Scripture?

But I do not wish to fight a man of straw. Unquestionably, Spenser translated the *Song of Songs* into English verse. The exact form is immaterial. Any rendition of the poem must have plunged one so responsive to aesthetic subtleties into an intensive examination of this strange song of love; and baffled though he might have been at its mysterious cadences, he might well have perceived the artistic principle that shaped its exotic imagery. Or failing this, the great word-painter must have absorbed so deeply into his poetic heart the magnificent pictures of the lyric that he apprehended this creative principle unconsciously and instinctively. Certainly one case or the other is true; for here and there, various of his poems bear the unmistakable impress of the spirit, if not the letter, of the imagery of *Canticum Canticorum*.

Little is known about Spenser's debt to this imagery. Commentary from Upton onwards has presented a few oft-repeated stylistic similarities in the form of analogues, parallels, or tentative sources. None to the writer's knowledge has gone beyond this stage of investigation. Those debts of the spirit—and these constitute the major part of the debt—have been overlooked; the extent and nature of the influence have never been studied as a unit. These matters still remain to be determined. The assembly of all the "suspicious" images enables one to demonstrate that in an ultimate sense, Spenser's *"Canticum canticorum* translated" is not completely lost, even though its original form seems irrevocably gone. It still lives, though without its name,[7] in a few passages of the *Epithalamion,* the *Amoretti,* the *Faerie Queene,* and *Colin*

---

of Poesie maintained that *"Salomon*...wrate in meeters...although to many... ignorant of the Hebrue language and phrase, and not obseruing it, the same seeme but like a prose" (*Ibid.,* II, 10); later, Milton, agreeing with Origen, found the "Song of *Salomon*" "a divine pastoral Drama...consisting of two persons and a double *Chorus*" (*Critical Essays of the Seventeenth Century,* ed. J. E. Spingarn, I, 196). In a study still unpublished I explain in detail these and many other evaluations of Hebrew poetry in Renaissance criticism.

[7] P. M. Buck's suggestion ("Spenser's Lost Poems," *PMLA*, XXIII [1908], 80-89) that some of the lost poems may be found under new names in his extant work, does not include *Canticum Canticorum*.

Clouts Come Home Againe. The voice is faint, /25/ and the spirit flickers but feebly, yet close attention will discover them.[8]

It is but natural to look first at the *Epithalamion*. What is the reward? A passage bearing the distinctive stamp of the scriptural epithalamium. Buried amid the more conventional imagery of Spenser's marriage song we find the unusual simile,

> Her snowie necke lyke to a marble towre (*Epithal.*, 177).

In the biblical marriage song we read,

> Thy necke is like a tower of iuory (*Song of Sol.*, 7:5).

and

> Thy necke is as the tower of Dauid built for a defence
> (*Song of Sol.*, 4:4).[9]

The similarity in phrasing and imagery fairly leaps at you. So does the utter strangeness of Spenser's image. This exoticism is the resultant of an artistic principle peculiar to Oriental poetry; it embodies a specific clue to Spenser's debt to the *Song of Songs*. Thus, a brief analysis of this shaping principle and a demonstration of its relationship to that of the *Song of Solomon* is for the moment imperative.

The image is clearly un-Spenserian, un-Elizabethan, un-Occidental. To the Western imagination, it fails to create that illusion which is poetic truth. Despite the correspondences of line and color, the figures of neck and tower refuse to coalesce into a credible picture. The Western reader seizes upon the colossal disparity in proportions, the monstrous incongruity in size, and is tempted to smile. Not so the Oriental reader. He sees nothing ridiculous in the comparison, for his aesthetic realization is independent of close sensory congruity. His poetic /26/ tradition "combines with imagery, *the very different device of symbolism,*" an appeal "to some analytical faculty or conventional association of ideas" rather than to the pictorial sense.[10]

---

[8] I have used the most available contemporary text, the *Bishop's Bible* of 1568. A nice determination of Spenser's text is unnecessary here, because all contemporary versions, however they differ in allegorical interpretation, are virtually identical in the translation of the imagery of this poem. Moreover, Spenser's is chiefly a debt of the spirit, not of the letter.

[9] Archbishop Parker, ed. *Bishop's Bible* (London, 1568). All biblical references are to this text.

[10] R. G. Moulton, *A Modern Reader's Bible* (New York, 1920), pp. 1448–1450. The general exposition of the imagery of *Canticles* is indebted to Moulton's analysis.

The tower is a symbol to him—a symbol of excellence, a recognized standard of value. It is a "tower of David"; it is "built for a defence"; "a thousand shields hang therein, and all the targates of the strong men" (v.4). That is to say, it is a tower par excellence, an object raised to transcendent value through glorious historic and functional associations, which the contemporary reader will immediately perceive. That strength and security, shields and bucklers cannot be transferred metaphorically to the Shulamite maid's neck is as obvious to him as it is to us; but he does not attempt to make the transfer. Apparently his analytic approach so modifies the sensory effect of the comparison, that the physical and qualitative incongruities are blurred or obscured or ignored. He rivets his attention upon the transference of value, or preeminent quality to the body of the girl, and upon "the ingenuity of the comparison."[11] Knowing that the poet is not attempting to paint a picture of the girl's body, but to identify it with excellence, his imagination is perfectly satisfied with the most shadowy, the most partial, the most superficial physical or qualitative correspondence to the standard of value. Thus, purely because of their correspondence in color and line, lips become a thread of scarlet (4:3); because of the resemblance in whiteness and eveness, teeth become a flock of newly shorn ewes just come from the washing, all of them paired and none missing (4:2). Here "nothing is painted; there is simply a reference to supreme types of excellence."[12] The thread and the ewes are merely symbols. So with the figures of speech regularly used for the sexual relations—"the vineyard, the garden shut up and the fountain sealed ... the sport of the roe amongst the lilies or upon the 'mountains of separation'; in all these there is no realism, but its opposite, conventional substitutes for vivid expressions."[13] The figure, then, is symbolic; it is not materially identified with the body. It is an ingenious vehicle of qualitative transference; nothing more. /27/

The *Song of Songs* has one distinctive variation of symbolism—the groupings of excellences. The aesthetic effect is built up, not by the isolation of any one detail, but by the combined suggestiveness of all. "The comparison must be made with the group as a whole ... the mind must gather from the whole the complete suggestiveness"[14] of the passage. Individual parts of the body are enumerated and frankly described in a rapid-fire succession of images, but the individual images blend into a sensory unity unmatched in the corporeal descriptions of Spenser's

---

[11] *Ibid.*
[12] *Ibid.*
[13] *Ibid.*
[14] *Ibid.*, p. 1449.

period, say, in the sensuality of *Venus and Adonis,* or *Hero and Leander,* or Acrasia's Bower of Bliss on the one hand, and the veritable anaesthesia of the conventional sonnets on the other. Since in the *Song of Songs,* physical congruity is irrelevant and the sensory focus falls upon the ingenious symbol rather than on the part of the body, this new unity resolves itself into a pure fusion of symbols. Amid the combined sensuous association of the figures, the parts of the body are obscured. "To the imagination, it [the imagery] acts rather as a sedative than a stimulus . . . and is itself a form of reserve; it can handle topics which more realistic writing must leave alone" if the realism is not meant to be erogenic.[15] Thus, the grouping of values here generates an appeal that is tremendously sensuous but utterly non-sensual.

Illustration by quotation and contrast will clarify the point:

> My wel beloued is white and ruddy . . .
> His head is as fine golde, his lockes curled and blacke as a rauen.
> His eyes are like doues upon riuers of waters, which are washt
> with milke, and remain by the ful vessels.
> His cheekes are as a bedde of spices, and as sweete flowers,
> and his lippes like lilies dropping down pure myrrhe.
> His handes as rings of golde set with crysolite, his belly like
> white yuory couered with saphirs.
> His legges are as pillars of marble, set upon sockets of fine golde;
> his countenance as Lebanon, excellent of the ceder.
> His mouth is as sweete things: and he is wholly delectable.
>
> (*Song of Sol.*, 5:10–16)

The virtually complete absence of realism is apparent. For example, "His head is as fine golde, his lockes . . . blacke as a rauen," if viewed in terms other than symbolical, is contra/28/dictory; the double suggestiveness blurs the picture. However, as symbols of two different aspects of beauty, they are supplementary. With the inventory of the remaining corporeal components, they constitute a fusion of excellences whose total effect is highly sensuous but definitely not erogenic— "white," "ruddy," "fine golde," "blacke as a rauen," "washt with milke," "white yuory couered with saphirs," "pillars of marble set upon sockets of fine golde," appealing to the visual sense; "bedde of spices," "sweete flowers," "lilies dropping down pure myrrhe," to the olfactory sense; "His cheekes are as a bedde of spices and as sweete flowers," to the sense of taste; and all losing their individual identities in the combined suggestiveness of the group. The reference to the treasured minerals and to

---

[15] *Ibid.,* p. 1450.

the scents of the field and country should be carefully noted, for they are marked characteristics of Spenser's *Canticum Canticorum* vein.

Appeal to the senses is, of course, common to virtually all poetry. But the piling up of a profusion of images in such a short passage; the use of the symbols; the description of various parts of the body in an unbroken succession of similes; and the peculiarly sensuous effect of the combination are distinctly not of the Elizabethan tradition. One phase of that tradition, the sonnet literature of love, presents a contrast in method which is sufficiently striking to speak for itself:

> Sweet warriour, when shall I haue peace with you?
>   High time it is, this warre now ended were:
>   which I no lenger can endure to sue,
>   ne your incessant battry more to beare:
> So weake my powres, so sore my wounds appeare,
>   that wonder is that I should liue a iot,
>   seeing my hart through launched euery where
>   with thousand arrowes, which your eyes haue shot:
> Yet shoot ye sharpely still, and spare me not,
>   but glory thinke to make these cruel stoures.
>   ye cruell one, what glory can be got,
>   in slaying him that would liue gladly yours?
> Make peace therefore, and graunt me timely grace,
>   that al my wounds wil heale in little space.
>
>   (*Amoretti*, LVII)

This sonnet, representing one of the strongest conventions of amatory poetry and typifying some forty of Spenser's poems,[16] has none of the characteristics of the passage above: neither the /29/ succession of similes, nor the listing of parts of the body, nor an appreciable sensory appeal, nor least of all, the symbolism. The sweet warrior comparison is intellectual in conception. Its purpose is "wit," the fantastic riding of a single metaphor through an involved path to a clever conclusion. The lady is a warrior, not because she resembles one superficially, or partially, or even symbolically, but because a literary tradition had established the convention of the cruel mistress and had challenged virtuosity to elaborate the sweet warrior paradox. In this tradition, the more complicated the metaphor and the more successfully dialectic dexterity pursued it to an ingenious conclusion, the more successful the poem. But such description, however much its verbal jugglery titillates the intellect, does not stir the senses with images of loveliness. How differ-

---

[16] Cf. sonnets 10–12, 14, 18–26, 29–38, 41–44, 46–58.

Epithalamion

ent from Spenser's garden sonnet, or the jewel sonnet, or other descriptions to be quoted shortly.

Another contrast with the *Song of Songs* involving the same general principle is the paradox of love convention[17] as embodied in the ice and fire formula. A few lines suffice to refresh the memory.

> My loue is lyke to yse, and I to fyre;
>   how comes it then that this her cold so great
>   is not dissolu'd through my so hot desyre,
>   but harder growes the more I her intreat?
> Or how comes it that my exceeding heat
>   is not delayd by her hart frosen cold:
>   but that I burne much more in boyling sweat,
>   and feele my flames augmented manifold?
>   (*Amoretti*, XXX, 1-8)

A further contrast to the rhapsodic praise of physical perfection in the *Song of Songs* is Spenser's impassioned expression of the neoplatonic "idea" of beauty in some fifteen sonnets.[18] If the preceding sonnets ignore an inventory of intimate physical loveliness, these poems negate the conception of the physical as an object of praise. Two selections are sufficient to point the contrast.

> Within my hart, though hardly it can shew
>   thing so diuine to vew of earthly eye, /30/
>   the fayre Idea of your celestiall hew,
>   and euery part remaines immortally:
>   (*Amoretti*, XLV, 5-8)

> Ne ought I see, though in the clearest day,
>   when others gaze upon theyre shadowes vayne:
>   but th' onely image of that heauenly ray,
>   whereof some glance doth in mine eie remayne.
> Of which beholding the Idaea playne,
>   through contemplation of my purest part:
>   with light thereof I doe myselfe sustayne,
>   and thereon feed my loue-affamisht hart.
>   (*Amoretti*, LXXXVIII, 5-12)

In the last selection, Spenser disavows the physical completely.

Except for those sonnets conferring immortality upon the mistress through the poet's verse,[19] these represent in general Spenser's typical

---

[17] Cf. sonnets 30, 35, 42.
[18] Cf. sonnets 3, 8, 13, 45, 55, 61, 66, 68, 79, 80, 83, 84, 85, 88.
[19] Cf. sonnets 27, 69, 75, 82.

treatments of his beloved. These comprehend about 55 of his 89 sonnets in the *Amoretti* sequence. The others, aside from those bearing the Oriental strain, are hard to classify; but in the whole sequence, the typical picture is the conventional bright beam, the golden hair, the heavenly ray, the wings of love, the battery of arrows, Daphne, Phoebus, Cupid, the storm, the tossed ship, and so on. Only when Spenser shows the influence of the *Song of Songs* does he desert these familiar patterns to describe his mistress intimately and sensuously.

On the other hand, in *The Faerie Queene,* the descriptions of women are often intimate and more than sensuous. But these, representing the opposite pole of the Elizabethan tradition, differ sharply from those of the *Song of Songs*. First, they are confined almost exclusively to wanton creatures like Phaedria, Acrasia, Acrasia's damsels, or the earthly Venus; they are never used for Elizabeth in any of her guises or for women of modesty. Second, they are not developed by the series of lofty symbols, but by a combination of conventional images and suggestive pictures of the body in lascivious motions or seen through revealing garments or some form of disarray. When upon occasion a loose form of bodily inventory is given, Spenser falls back upon such conventionalities as alabaster skin, snowy breast, fair locks, golden wire, fiery beams, crystalline humor, and many classical allusions. The descriptions of the damsels in the Bower of Bliss,[20] of Acrasia, and of Phaedria demonstrate /31/ the poet's method here. Even the effect of

---

[20] Space limits me to one quotation. The others are merely cited. "Two naked Damzelles he therein espyde/ which therein bathing, seemed to contend,/ And wrestle wantonly, ne car'd to hyde,/ Their dainty parts from vew of any which them eyde./ Sometimes the one would lift the other quight/ Aboue the waters, and then downe againe/ Her plong, as ouer maistered by might,/ Where both awhile would couered remaine,/ ... The whiles their snowy limbes, as through a vele,/ So through the Christall waues appeared plaine:/ Then suddeinly both would themselues vnhele,/ And th' amarous sweet spoiles to greedy eyes reuele,/ As that faire Starre, the messenger of morne,/ His deawy face out of the sea doth reare:/ Or, as the *Cyprian* goddesse, newly borne/ Of th' Oceans fruitfull froth, did first appeare:/ Such seemed they, and so their yellow heare/ Christalline humour dropped downe apace./ ... One her selfe low ducked in the flood,/ ... th' other rather higher did arise,/ and her two lilly paps aloft displayd,/ And all, that might his melting hart entise/ To her delights, she vnto his bewrayd;/ The rest hid vnderneath, him more desirous made./ With that, the other likewise vp arose,/ And her faire lockes .../ she low adowne did lose:/ Which flowing long and thick, her cloth'd arownd,/ ... So that faire spectacle from him was reft,/ Yet that, which reft it, no lesse faire was fownd:/ So hid in lockes and waues from lookers theft .../ Now when they spide the knight to slacke his pace,/ Them to behold, and in his sparkling face/ The secret signes of kindled lust appeare,/ Their wanton meriments they did encreace,/ And to him beckned, to approch more neare,/ And shewd him many sights, that courage cold could reare."/ (*FQ*, II, 12, 63–68). Cf. also II, 5, 32–33; II, 12, 55; II, 12, 77–78; Phaedria, II, 6, 3–11; II, 6, 21; II, 12, 14–16.

such descriptions as those of the modest Diana and Britomart[21] is attained largely through revealing dishabille. The other details in these cases, as in the description of Pastorella—her "golden haire," "snowy brest," "yuory chest"[22]—are thoroughly conventional and unaphrodisiac. These examples and those of the sonnets constitute representative samples of Spenser's normal modes of describing feminine beauty. Utterly distinct from them is his *Song of Songs* technique which we found in that almost literal refrain, the text of the foregoing analysis,—"Her snowie necke lyke to a marble towre."

Commentators have noted this refrain before, but they have failed to establish its debt by their failure to recognize that this image is merely the last of *a group of pictures* created in the spirit of *Canticum Canticorum*. The poet describes his bride thus:

> Tell me ye merchants daughters did ye see
> So fayre a creature in your towne before,
> So sweet, so louely, and so mild as she,
> Adornd with beautyes grace and vertues store, /32/
> Her goodly eyes lyke Saphyres shining bright,
> Her forehead yuory white,
> Her cheekes lyke apples which the sun hath rudded,
> Her lips lyke cherryes charming men to byte,
> Her brest like to a bowle of creame vncrudded,
> Her paps lyke lyllies budded,
> Her snowie necke lyke to a marble towre.
> (*Epithal.*, ll. 167–177)

The similarity between the opening and that of *Amoretti* XV, to be quoted later, where the merchants are virtually identified as traders with the East, and where the same listing of physical treasures are followed, arouses immediate suspicions. The character of the similes confirms these suspicions: first and foremost by the tower image, which is an indisputable refrain of the *Song of Songs*; and second by the frank inventory of corporeal parts through the now familiar succession of short symobls which unite to blur the body and hence to prevent the stimulation of erotic emotion. It is true that at least two of the images— the sapphire and cherry—are *per se* conventional; but it is no less true that they are imbedded in and constitute part of a group of symbols whose highly un-Spenserian spirit imposes upon all the members a dis-

---

[21] *FQ*, III, 6, 18–19; III, 9, 20–21; IV, 1, 13–14.
[22] *FQ*, VI, 9, 9 and VI, 12, 15.

tinctly exotic coloring. This coloring is far removed from the word-play of the sweet warrior and the ice and fire poems; from the negation of the material in the platonic sonnets; from the eroticism of *The Faerie Queene* pictures. But it does stir sensory stimuli of a sedative character by virtue of the unrealistic, the symbolic nature of the standards of value which carry the focus of the portrait.

Let us examine one other simile beside that of the tower echo of the *Song of Songs*—"Her brest like to a bowle of creame vncrudded." As a pictorial comparison it is ridiculous; the metaphorical transfer gags the Western poetic will-to-believe. But as an identification of the breast with a supreme symbol of whiteness and purity, the simile is in complete figurative harmony with the tower-like neck and the lily-like paps. Nor can this spirit be explained away as an influence of Theocritus. "All the points of contact between the two collections of songs [the *Idyls* and the *Song of Songs*] may be explained as due to their /33/ having been composed at the same period under similar conditions of environment."[23] The existence of the tower debt to *The Book of Canticles,* the singular technique of the image, the successive visual appeals of sapphires, white ivory, red apples, lips like cherries, bowl of cream, marble tower, and the olfactory and saporific stimuli of apples, cherries, and lilies, all combine to demonstrate the biblical imagistic paternity of this passage.

Even stronger evidence of the same influence is presented by *Amoretti,* XV, although it has never been cited in this connection:[24]

---

[23] Paul Haupt, *The Book of Canticles* (Chicago, 1902), pp. 17–18.
[24] The influences of Phillipe Desportes' "Diane" I, IXXXII, has been noted here by commentators, but a comparison of the *specific application of the images to bodily attributes* shows no similarity. The inference is plain that though Spenser may have been influenced by the treasure concept of Desportes, his peculiar use of the imagery was not. It was dictated by the artistic principle of the *Song of Songs.* The sonnet reads:

> Marchands, qui recherchez tout le rivage more
> Du froid septentrion, et qui sans reposer,
> A cent mille dangers vous allez exposer,
> Pour un gain incertain, qui vos esprits dévore,
> Venez seulement voir la beauté que j'adore,
> Et par quelle richesse elle a sçeu m'attiser:
> Et je suis seur qu'après vous ne pourrez priser
> Le plus rare trésor dont l'Afrique se dore.
> Voyez les filets d'or de ce chef blondissant,
> L'éclat de ces rubis, ce coral rougissant,
> Ce cristal, cet ébène, et ces graces divines,
> Cet argent, cet yvoire, et ne vous contentez
> Qu'on ne vous montre encor mille autres raretez
> Mille beaux diamans et mille perles fines.

> Ye tradefull Merchants, that with weary toyle,
>> do seeke most pretious things to make your gain;
>> and both the Indias of their treasures spoile,
>> what needeth you to seeke so far in vaine?
> For loe my loue doth in her selfe containe
>> all this worlds riches that may farre be found.
>> If Saphyres, loe her eies be Saphyres plaine,
>> if Rubies, loe hir lips be Rubies sound:
> If Pearles, hir teeth be pearles both pure and round;
>> if Yuorie, her forehead yuory weene;
>> if Gold, her locks are finest gold on ground;
>> if Siluer, her faire hands are siluer sheene.
>
> (*Amoretti*, XV, 1-12) /34/

The figures are a far cry from those of the sonnets recorded above. Unquestionably, they issue from the imagistic principle of such similes as

> His head is as fine golde,
> His handes as rings of golde set with crysolite,
> His belly like white yuory couered with saphirs,
> His legges are as pillars of marble, set upon sockets of fine golde.
>
> (*Song of Sol.*, 5:11, 14, 15)

Here, first, is the familiar grouping of supreme excellences through symbols whose effect is to be grasped only if the comparison be made with the whole group rather than with the individual details. The girl's body, through the suggestiveness of the complete passage, has ceased to be flesh and blood; it has been translated into a veritable treasure house of Eastern jewels. Inextricably interwoven with the first characteristic is the inventory of the body in the unbroken parallelism. Finally, the nature of the symbols themselves shows the mark of the *Song of Solomon*.

Take, for example, the teeth-pearl parallel. As the sapphire is invoked as a symbol for blueness of the eye, so is the pearl for whiteness of the teeth. But as in the tower comparison, a distortion arises if the metaphor be tested primarily by realistic likness and the symbolism be disregarded. For though "pure" pearls, unmodified by another adjective, may evoke a picture of beautiful teeth, "round" pearls, certainly do not. Such a qualification, interpreted in the Occidental tradition, snaps the willing suspension of disbelief. It renders the comparison an absurdity. "Round" pearls added to "pure" ones, however, do give a faithful representation of *prefect* pearls. The image constitutes a superlative symbol of a form of beauty embodying the perfection not only of color, but of line and texture. Perfect teeth, of course, resemble round pearls no more closely than "pillars of marble, set upon sockets of fine golde" resemble legs. In each case there is at least one added factor—"round" and "sockets of fine golde," respectively,—which are fatal to Western credulity. But as "pillars of marble, *set upon sockets of fine golde*," represent to the biblical poet a value far above the common pillar, so do the "pearles both pure and *round*" represent to Spenser a value far above that of the ordinary pearl. Unless we are to accuse a superb painter of a sudden visual /35/ obtuseness which pursued him through at least two other pictures in this sonnet, we are forced to the conclusion that his extraordinary technique is here moved by his desire to direct the reader's attention to the standards of value rather than to the members of the body, to the interfusing connotations of the high symbols rather than to the eyes, the teeth, the locks, the forehead, and the hands themselves.

The same method is exemplified in the identification of the girl's locks with the *"finest* gold on *ground."* It is significant that this figure for golden hair is the only use of its kind in Spenser. There is a sufficiency of golden wire and golden locks, and so on, but not a single simile or metaphor of this kind. The imagery here is neither conventional nor realistic. Its sole function is to suggest beauty, as in the neck-tower and the teeth-round pearl figures, in symbols of transcendent value. Thus the girl's hair is objectified, not as gold spun into fine threads, but as the precious ore itself—"the *finest* gold on ground,"—an image grotesque from any view save the symbolic, but sufficiently reminiscent in principle and phrasing of "his head is as *fine* golde" to justify the assumption of scriptural influence. Spenser pursues the same objective when he identifies her hands with "siluer sheene," an unusual and unrealistic comparison comparable to the biblical "his handes as rings of golde."

There is more of the same stamp in the description of Mirabella:

> Her yuorie necke, her alabaster brest,
> Her paps, which like white silken pillowes were,
> For loue in soft delight thereon to rest;
> Her tender sides, her bellie white and clere,
> Which like an Altar did it selfe vprere,
> To offer sacrifice diuine thereon;
> Her goodly thighes, whose glorie did appeare
> Like a triumphall Arch, and thereupon
>> The spoiles of Princes hang'd, which were in battel won.
>
> (*FQ*, VI, 8, 42)

Epithalamion 93

The last three lines are indisputably influenced in symbolism, and with a slight variation, in imagery, by

> Thy necke is as the tower of Dauid built for a defence; a thousand shields hang therein, and all the targates of the strong men.
> (*Song of Sol.*, 4:4)

The inconsequential difference in imagery is Spenser's substitution of "thighes" and "Arch" for "necke" and "tower." The /36/ imagerial correspondence between the rest of the two similes—"and thereupon/The spoiles of Princes hang'd, which were in battel won" and "a thousand shields hang therein, and all the targates of the strong men"—is too striking to admit anything short of indebtedness. The image of the arch, as well as those preceding, "paps" for "white silken pillowes," and especially "sides" and "bellie" for an "Altar," can be correctly apprehended only as a symbol. Surely, Spenser is not striving for realism; the picture of Mirabella as a combination of sacrificial altar and triumphal arch is ridiculous. He is glorifying Mirabella through standards of value; he is endowing her thighs with supreme beauty and glory by identifying them with an object resembling them in shape but transcending them in stature and in glorious associations. Thus, "the spoiles of Princes hang'd, which were in battel won," far from rendering the image a piece of verbal grotesquerie, actually heightens the power of the Oriental symbol. It makes the arch the *ne plus ultra* of arches; and by transference, the thighs the *ne plus ultra* of thighs.

Again in *The Faerie Queene,* a little area bears the same impress. The key passage describes Belphoebe's legs as "Like two faire marble pillours" (*FQ*, II, 3, 28, 1), an unmistakable echo of "His legges are as pillars of marble" (*Song of Sol.*, 5:15). The symbolism of the image needs no comment by this time. In lines 7 and 8 of the stanza immediately following we find

> Her daintie paps: which like young fruit in May
> Now little gan to swell.
> (*FQ*, II, 3, 29, 7-8)

It is indubitable that this passage was written under the spell of the biblical epithalamium; first, because of its proximity to the well-nigh literal borrowing of the "marble pillours"; and, second, because of Spenser's use of a similar image, "Her paps lyke lyllies budded," in a line from the *Epithalamion* immediately preceding the almost identical and certainly irrefutable refrain of the *Song of Songs*—"Her snowie necke lyke to a marble towre." This juxtaposition of similar images in two unusual passages is, I believe, more than sheer coincidence. It indicates that when a line from the *Song of Songs* echoed through the mysterious labyrinth of the poet's imagination, it was likely to carry with it other imagistic associations from the same poem. More-/37/over, as we shall see in a moment, one of the typical comparisons of the *Canticles*, much like the Spenser image, is

> . . . thy breastes shall be lyke clusters of the vine,
> (*Song of Sol.* 7:9)

a reference to fruits and flowers of field and country. Finally, we actually discover other similes whose metaphorical law is identical with that of the similes in the *Song of Songs*. In Stanza 24 we read:

> Her iuorie forhead, full of bountie braue,
> Like a broad table did it selfe dispred,
> For Loue his loftie triumphes to engraue.
> (*FQ*, II, 3, 24, 1–3)

Continuing from line 7, we find:

> Sweet words, like dropping honny she did shed,
> And twixt the perles and rubins softly brake
> A siluer sound . . .

Perhaps the last simile seems commonplace if regarded in isolation. Yet, in the light of the circumstance that the passage from Stanza 24 through 29 describing Belphoebe has undeniable associations with the *Song of Songs*, it is a probability treading the heels of certainty that, ringing unconsciously through Spenser's imagination, was the insistent *Song of Songs* motif of the sweetness of the lover's voice and words and lips, such as the honey simile in 4:11, "Thy lippes, my spouse, droppe as hony-combes; hony and milk are under thy tongue," a reference to speech as well as to kisses; or 5:13, ". . . and his lippes like lilies dropping downe pure myrrhe;" or 5:16, "His mouth is as sweet things," or 2:14, ". . . for thy voyce is sweet . . . ."[25]/38/

---

[25] Upton (*Spenser's Faerie Queene* [1758], II, 444–45) and Todd (*The Works of Edmund Spenser* [1805], III, 304–311), corroborate this contention about the figures of the Belphoebe description except the "iuory forhead-broad table" simile. Their failure and the failure of subsequent editors to see the symbolism here accounts, as it does with regard to all the unnoticed previous references I have cited, for the omission of this passage from the debts to *Canticum Canticorum*. Both editors, however, Todd following Upton, push the biblical influence back further than I insist

Epithalamion

The belief that *The Book of Canticles* inspired the honey simile (and with it, the table figure which it follows and the pillar figure just four stanzas later) is materially fortified by the presence of a kindred image in another description of Elizabeth—this time in *Colin Clouts Come Againe,* where we find

> Her words were like a streame of honny fleeting,
> The which doth softly trickle from the hiue. (596-597)

This is followed by

> Her deeds were like great clusters of ripe grapes,
> Which load the braunches of the fruitfull vine . . .
> Her lookes were like beames of the morning Sun,
> Forth looking through the windowes of the East . . .
> Her thoughts are like the fume of Franckincence,
> Which from a golden Censer forth doth rise. . . . (600-605, 608-609)

In this last passage a search for verbal identities would be fruitless. There are none. The morning sun simile merely illustrates the Eastern coloring of the passage; deeds in the *Song of Songs* are never grapes nor are thoughts frankincense. But we do not expect to find Spenser lifting images bodily out of the *Song of Songs* to deposit them unmodified into his own poetry. It is sufficient evidence of his debt to the imagery of that poem to find him synthesizing the stuff of experience into pictures that are kindred spiritually; to find his imagination creating the same species of combinations which distinguish the biblical marriage song; to find in his lines the same kind of symbolism and the same kind of visual, olfactory and saporific imagery of the *grapes,* the *clusters,* the *vine,* and the *incense* that characterizes

> thy breasts are lyke clusters of grapes, (*Song of Sol.,* 7:8),
> thy breasts shall now be lyke clusters of the vine, (7:9),
> Let us get up early to the vines, let us see if the vine flourisheth, whether it hath budded the small grapes, (7:13),
> I will get me to the mountain of myrrhe and to the hill of Frankincense, (4:6),

---

upon—to the quite conventional red and white figure in Stanza 22, where Belphoebe's face is "... withouten blame or blot/ Through goodly mixture of complexions dew;/ And in her cheekes the vermeill red did shew/ Like roses in a bed of lillies shed/" (*FQ,* II, 3, 22, 3-6), citing *Canticles* 2:1; 4:7; 5:9. (Upton, *op. cit.,* II, 444.)

> Who is shee that commeth out of the Wilderness lyke pillars of smoke perfumed with myrrhe and incense and with all the spices of the marchant, (3:6),
> Thy plants are as an orchard . . . with the trees of incense, (4:13–14).

The things described by Spenser are different; the terms of the description are the same. The inference is irresistible that the Spenser passages here were influenced by the luxuriant imagery of the *Song of Songs*. /39/

This luxuriance, it will be observed, is due largely to the symbolic use of field and garden images. Such a method of portraiture evidently impressed Spenser deeply, for it reveals its influence in his "garden" sonnet, where again, as in his treasure sonnet, he groups excellences through a series of parallel standards of value. In the treasure lyric, the mistress was transformed into an ideal represented by the brilliance and richness of priceless jewels. In *Song of Songs* 5:10–16,[26] she became all that vision, taste, and smell can give of sensuous beauty. In the following passage she has become all that the savor and odor of the feast can give of delight:

> How much better is thy loue then wine? and the sauour of thine oyntments then all spices? Thy lippes, my Spouse, droppe as honycombes: hony and milke are under thy tongue, and the sauour of thy garment is as the sauour of Lebanon.
> (*Song of Sol.*, 4:10–11)[27]

In the next quotation, through the use of a single type of symbols, the girl's body has been transmuted into all the interfused fragrance of the garden:

> Thy plants are as an orchard of pomegranates with sweet fruits, as camphire, spikenard.
> Even spikenard and saffron: calamus, and cynamon, with the trees of incense, myrrhe and aloes, with all the chief spices.
> O Fountaine of the gardens, O well of liuing waters, and the springs of Lebanon.
> Arise, O North, and come, O South, and blow on my garden, that the spices thereof may flow out: let my wel beloued come to his garden, and eat his pleasant fruit.
> (*Song of Sol.*, 4:13–16)

---

[26] Cf. pp. 6–7.
[27] Moulton, *op. cit.*, p. 1449.

So, in Spenser's "garden sonnet," his "wel beloued" has become the intermingled fragrance of a garden.

> Comming to kisse her lyps, (such grace I found)
>   Me seemd I smelt a gardin of sweet flowres:
>   that dainty odours from them threw around
>   for damzels fit to decke their louers bowres.
> Her lips did smell lyke vnto Gillyflowers,
>   her ruddy cheekes lyke vnto Roses red:
>   her snowy browes lyke buddled Bellamoures,
>   her louely eyes lyke Pincks but newly spred.
> Her goodly bosome lyke a Strawberry bed,
>   her neck lyke to a bounch of Cullambynes: /40/
>   her brest lyke lillyes, ere theyr leaues be shed,
>   her nipples lyke yong blossomd Iessemynes.
> Such fragrant flowres doe giue most odorous smell,
>   but her sweet odour did them all excell.
>
>   (*Amoretti*, LXIIII)

The beauty of this passage derives, like that of the garden passage of *Canticles*, not from the singling out of details, but from the sensuous and sedative suggestiveness of the whole group; and though there are no exact parallels in olfactory imagery between the two poems, the technique and the general flavor of the descriptions are singular enough to cast the strongest of suspicions upon the source of Spenser's inspiration. Contrast the naive, unelaborated character of the short similes of this sonnet with the utterly sophisticated and elaborated conceits of the "sweet warriour" and "ice and fire" sonnets; the total lack of sensuousness in these and in the Platonic sonnets with the aromatic richness of this garden poem; the absence of the inventory of corporeal members in these three poems with the garden poem; and compare with this garden sonnet such passages possessing the fragrance, the frankness, the short simile, and cataloguing as "thy breastes shall now be lyke clusters of the vine, and the sauour of thy nose like apples," or "His cheekes are as a bedde of spices, and as sweet flowers," or "My spikenard sent forth its fragrance/My wel-beloued is a bundle of myrrhe unto me . . . /My wel-beloued is a cluster of camphire unto me in the vines of Engedy," or "I am the rose of the field, and the lilie of the valleyes./Lyke a lilie among the thornes, so is my loue among the daughters," (*Song of Sol.*, 7:9; 5:13; 1:12–13; 2:1–2) and we are compelled to admit that Spenser's tone and method present a similarity so striking as to suggest strongly, in the light of previously established contacts, one more debt to the *Book of Canticles*.

This contention is strengthened by the reappearance of the garden simile in proximity to several comparisons which are unmistakably of coinage of the *Song of Solomon*. Moreover, this simile offers a clue to the character of the succeeding comparisons. Two previously cited examples involving an almost literal debt to the *Song of Songs*—"Her paps lyke lyllies budded,/Her snowie necke lyke to a marble towre," (*Epithal.*, 176–177) and "Her dainty paps; which like young fruit in May/Now little gan to swell," (*FQ*, II, 3, 29, 7–8) just one stanza away from /41/ "Like two faire marble pillours they were seene," (*FQ*, II, 3, 28, 1) show that the presence of the garden is a key to the new kind of imagery. In this particular case, the picture,

> And twixt her paps like early fruit in May,/ whose haruest seemd to hasten now apace (*Amoretti*, LXXVI, 9–10),

is almost identical with the one lying so close to the line, "Like two faire marble pillours they were seene," which even the most captious must admit to be an infiltration from the *Song of Songs*. And this image is not merely an accidental flash. It is prophetic of a little oasis in the desert of Occidental imagery—of an immediately succeeding sonnet where the comparison is symbolic and where physical perfections are painted in that exotic, sensuous, and sedative tone distinguishing the *Song of Songs*. Here in the maid's breast,

> A goodly table of pure yvory:/ all spred with iuncats, fit to entertayne/ the greatest Prince with pompus roialty (*Amoretti*, LXXVII, 2–4),

the color and purity of "pure yvory" are the sole elements of similarity. Obviously the function of the passage is to suggest by the connotative force of the symbol what *Canticles* 4:10–11, 13–16 with greater elaboration suggested—the intermingled delights of the banquet table. This design is borne out by the succeeding lines,

> Mongst which there in a siluer dish did ly/twoo golden apples of vnualewd price. (*Amoretti*, LXXVII, 5–6)

Patently, the "siluer dish" cannot even remotely suggest the human breast. It is purely a metaphorical standard of superlative beauty, which, with the preceding "pure yvory" and the succeeding and similarly symbolic "twoo golden apples of vnualewd price," must be interpreted in the spirit of "His belly like white yuory couered with saphirs" (*Song of Sol.*, 5:14), or "His legges are as pillars of marble, set upon sockets of fine golde" (*Song of Sol.*, 5:15), or even more aptly, "Thy nauel is lyke a round goblet wherein no mingled wine is wanting" (*Song of Sol.*, 7:3).

The apple metaphor should establish the case conclusively. Obviously the "twoo golden apples of vnualewd price" are the two breasts. Obviously, too, they are symbolic, not realistic images; *golden* cannot designate the color of breasts. Spenser /42/ uses the adjective because its literary associations suggest a supreme value. These golden apples are of unparagoned beauty, purity, and savor. They are

> far passing those which Hercules came by,
> or those which Atalanta did entice.
> Exceeding sweet, yet voyd of sinfull vice,
> That many sought yet none could euer taste,
> sweet fruit of pleasure brought from paradice,
> by loue himselfe, and in his garden plaste. (*Ibid.*, 7–12)

Golden apples, then renderd superlative through mythological associations, are set in a silver dish, on a table of pure ivory all spread with sweetmeats. Here is the intimate description of the body through symbols which deprive the image of erogenic qualities; the focus of the picture is the banquet-table, not the girl's body. Here, moreover, is the jewel symbolism—gold, silver, ivory, and the olfactory and saporific imagery—sweetmeats and apples. Here, finally, is the familiar grouping of values. Just as the body of the sonnet mistress became a treasure house of jewels and a garden of flowers, so in this poem her breast has been transfigured into the delicacies of a banquet table in the manner of the previously cited *Song of Songs*, 4:10–11.

This examination ends, as it began, with the two epithalamia. Strains of the biblical hymn reappear in the *Epithalamion* in two more passages. In the *Song of Songs* we read

> Arise, my loue, my faire one and come thy way
> For behold winter is past, the raine is changed, and is gone away,
> The flowers appear in the earth; the time of the singing birds is come and the voyce of the turtle doue is heard in our land . . .
> Arise, my loue, my faire one, and come away.
> My doue . . .
>
> (*Song of Sol.*, 2:10–13)[28] /43/

In the *Epithalamion* we find

> Do ye awake, and with fresh lusty hed,
> Go to the bowre of my beloued loue,
> My truest turtle doue,
> Bid her awake, ...
>
> (*Epithal.*, 22–25)

> Bid her awake therefore and soon her dight
> For lo the wished day is come at last ... (*Ibid.*, 30–31)

> ... my fayre loue of lillyes and roses (*Ibid.*, 43)

> Wake now my loue, awake; (*Ibid.*, 74)

Even though the pervasive influence of the Catullan model upon the lyric treatment and general development of the *Epithalamion*[29] is freely admitted, the subtle interweaving of biblical strands is perceptible here too. The turtle dove, the symbol of conjugal fidelity, is seldom used in the classics, and Van Winkle admits its possible ultimate derivation from the *Song of Songs*,[30] where it is used no less than six times.[31] Moreover, in the classical epithalamium, the wedding ceremony occurs in winter.[32] The time in the *Song of Songs* is spring or summer; Spenser's wedding was in midsummer.[33] If the phrasing of the adjurations, "do ye awake" and "bid her awake" has no *distinctively* biblical flavor, it is at least paralleled by the language of *Canti-*

---

[28] Note the possible influence of this passage upon *Amoretti* LXX. All italics are mine.

> Fresh *spring* the herald of loues mighty king,
> In whose cote armour richly are displayd
> *all sorts of flowers the which on earth do spring*
> ... *Goe to my loue*, where she is carelesse layd,
> Yet in her winters bowre not well awake:
> ... *Bid her therefore her selfe soone ready make*,
> ... *Make hast therefore sweet loue* ...

The adjurations, "goe to my loue," "bid her ... soone ready make," "make hast ... sweet loue," are epithalamic in tone, much like "Arise, my loue, my faire one, and come thy way." The references to the passing of winter and to the advent of spring with its flowers are similar too. It may be significant that this sonnet comes almost immediately after his beloved's surrender.

[29] C. Van Winkle, *Epithalamion* (New York, 1926), p. 26.
[30] *Ibid.*
[31] 1:15; 2:14; 4:1; 5:2; 5:12; 6:9.
[32] Van Winkle, *op. cit.*, p. 21.
[33] *Ibid.*

Epithalamion

cles. Certainly, "my faire loue[34] of lillyes and roses"[35] is too potently reminiscent of the *Song of Songs* to be regarded as a mere accidental juxtaposition of phrases savoring of the Scriptural lyric. Finally, Van Winkle himself cites the Song of Solomon 2:10–13[36] in connection /44/ with the last line of the quotation as a parallel at least. This combination of circumstances forces the conclusion that this pasage invoking the maidens to awaken the bride is interpenetrated to some slight degree by the lover's invocations in the *Song of Songs*.

The last filament of the *Song of Songs*, the least perceptible of all, perhaps, in the fabric of the *Epithalamion*, is the lover's query

> Who is the same, which at my window peepes?
> Or whose is that faire face that shines so bright,
> Is it not Cinthia . . .?
> (*Epithal.*, 372–374)

In the biblical song, we read

> Who is shee that looketh forth as the morning, faire as the moone?
> (*Song of Sol.*, 6:10)

Note, first, that both passages are introduced by an interrogative "who" clause; and, second, that the reference is to the moon. The interrogative method of calling attention to an image of beauty is twice repeated in the *Song of Songs*[37] and might well have impressed a sensitive reader like Spenser. The latter's use of the moon, it is true, differs from that of the biblical hymn. He introduces Cynthia for purposes of invocation; but it is significant that of all the invocations—to Night, Silence, Juno, Hebe, Hymen, and the stars—to bless the night of love, this is the only one introduced in the question form. What is the implication? That when the cue came for the invocation to the moon, the epithalamic association of the scriptural song with the moon guided the poet's hand into a kindred interrogation. The circumstance that Spenser uses the moon for an invocation rather than for a comparison, does not prejudice the validity of the influence in any way. At this stage of the

---

[34] Cf. *Song of Sol.*, 1:15: "My loue, behold thou art faire; behold thou art faire"; 1:16: "My welbeloued, thou art faire"; 2:10: "My loue, my faire one"; 2:13: "My loue, my faire one"; 4:1: "Behold thou art faire, my loue, behold thou art faire"; 4:7: "Thou art all faire my loue"; 4:10: "How faire is thy loue"; 7:7: "How faire art thou, . . . oh my loue."

[35] Cf. *Song of Sol.*, 2:1; 2:2; 2:16; 6:3; 4:5; 5:10; 5:13; 6:2.

[36] Van Winkle, *op. cit.*, p. 89.

[37] Cf. 3:6: "Who is shee . . . ?" and 8:5: "Who is this . . . ?"

Epithalmion, the poet had ended the description of the bride; it was his turn to call upon Cynthia for assistance. The alchemy of poetic association did the rest.[38] /45/

I have ended with the most elusive of influences. I might have included others, but I am sensible of the danger of pressing into the realm of imponderables, which I have been skirting through much of this examination. After all, poetic imagery is an inexplicable imaginative synthesis which will not submit completely to human analysis. Spenser's imagination drew from a multiplicity of sources, and of these the *Song of Songs* was but a relatively shallow one. Hence, the task of separating such a minor component from a complex organic fusion has been hazardous and difficult; the imagery of the *Song of Songs* has not always precipitated clearly and purely. Many of the strains are faint. Few of the pictures conform closely to those in the scriptural song. But eight brief references carry the clear verbal imprint—*Epithalamion*, 176–177; *The Faerie Queene*, II, 3, 24, 7–8, II, 3, 28, 1, II, 3, 29, 7–8, VI, 8, 42, 7–9; *Colin Clouts Come Home Againe*, 596, 600 and 608–609. The remaining citations—*Epithalamion*, 22–25, 30–31, 43, 74, (possibly also 118–120) 167–175, and 372–374, *The Faerie Queene*, II, 3, 24, 1–3, VI, 8, 42, 1–6; *Amoretti*, XV, LXIIII, LXXVI 9–10, LXXVII 2–8 (and possibly the adjurations of LXX)—are interpenetrated with the distinctive technique and the characteristic flavor of the *Song of Songs*. These constitute Spenser's demonstrable debt. The ultimate conclusion must then be this—that the influence of the imagery of *Canticum Canticorum* upon Spenser's poetry, though admittedly small, is far greater than uninvestigated or conditional supposition would have it be; that it emerges now and then, sometimes nebulously, sometimes clearly, but always perceptibly, in the poet's two tributes to his

---

[38] A faint correspondence may be found between the *Epithalamion*, 118–120, and the *Song of Solomon*, 1:6. In the former, the groom, awaiting the bridal procession, pleads with the sun not to mar the fairness of his bride's face, thus:

> "...let thy lifull heat not feruent be
> For feare of burning her sunshiny face,
> Her beauty to disgrace."

In the latter, during the procession itself, the bride apologizes for the "disgrace" which the "feruent" sun has worked upon her fairness:
"Regard yee me not that I am blacke; that the sun hath looked upon me."
She is swarthy because "the sonnes of my mother were against me; they made me the keeper of the vines...." The desideratum of fairness, of course, is characteristic of most courtly poetry, but the combination of kindred circumstances—the wedding day, the connection with the bridal processions, and the sun as the agent which destroys the fairness of complexion—constitutes an interesting analogue.

beloved, and in the descriptions of beautiful, chaste women in *The Faerie Queene* and *Colin Clouts Come Home Againe*; in fine, that Spenser's "*Canticum canticorum* translated" is veritably translated into a new, a highly fragmentary and shadowy, but discernible form in the pages of his extant poetry.

Language, Style

C. S. Lewis

From English Literature in the Sixteenth Century, Excluding Drama, *1954**

... those who wish to attack Spenser will be wise to concentrate on his style. There alone he is seriously vulnerable. I have made no attempt to conceal or defend those places where, on any view, he must be admitted to write dully, shrilly, or clumsily. But we come to something more controversial when we consider that quality which, in his best passages no less than in his worst, will alienate many modern readers— the absence of pressure or tension. There /392/ are, indeed, metrical variations, more numerous than we always remember. But the general effect is tranquil; line by line, unremarkable. His voice never breaks, he does not pluck you by the elbow, unexpected collocations of ideas do not pour out red hot. There is no irony or ambiguity. Some now would deny the name of poetry to writing of which this must be admitted. Let us not dispute about the name. It is more important to realize that this style (when it is true to itself) is suitable for Spenser's purpose. He needs to create a certain quiet in our minds. The great images, the embodiments, as I have said, of moods or whole phases of experience, rise best if we are not flurried. A still, brooding attention, not a perpetual excitment, is what he demands. It is also probably true that the lack of tension in his verse reflects the lack of tension in his mind. His poetry does not express (though of course it often presents) discord and struggle: it expresses harmony. No poet, I think, was ever less like an Existentialist. He discovered early what things he valued, and there is no sign that his allegiance ever wavered. He was of course often, perhaps usually, disappointed. The actual court did not conform to his standard of courtesy: mutability, if philosophically accepted

---

* From C. S. Lewis, *English Literature in the Sixteenth Century, Excluding Drama.* Oxford: Clarendon Press, 1954, pp. 391–393. Reprinted by permission of the publisher and the author.

from the outset, might yet prove unexpectedly bitter to the taste. But disappointment is not necessarily conflict. It did not for Spenser discredit the things of which he was disappointed. It might breed melancholy or indignation, but not doubt. Why, after all, should it? Spenser inherited the Platonic and Christian dualism: heaven was set over against earth, being against becoming, eternity against time. He knew from the outset that the lower, half-unreal world must always fail to copy its archetype exactly. The worst that experience could do was to show that the degree of failure was greater than one had anticipated. If he had thought that the objects of his desire were merely 'ideals', private, subjective, constructions of his own mind, then the actual world might have thrown doubt on those ideals. But he thought no such thing. The Existentialist feels *Angst* because he thinks that man's nature (and therefore his relation to all things) has to be created or invented, without guidance, at each moment of decision. Spenser thought that man's nature was given, discoverable, and discovered; he did not feel *Angst*. He was often sad: but not, at bottom, worried. To many of my readers such a state of mind must appear a total illusion. If they cannot suspend their disbelief, /393/ they should leave Spenser alone; there are plenty of other authors to read. They must not, however, suppose that he was under an illusion about the historical world. That is not where he differs from them. He differs from them in thinking that it is not the whole story. His tranquillity is a robust tranquillity that 'tolerates the indignities of time', refusing (if we may put the matter in his terms) to be deceived by them, recognizing them as truths, of 'a foolish world'. He would not have called himself 'the poet of our waking dreams': rather the poet of our waking.

Herbert David Rix

From Rhetoric in Spenser's Poetry, *1940**

/76/ Professor Leavis remarks that Milton in his Grand Style "seems to be... focussing rather upon words than upon perceptions, sensations, or things"; that he "exhibits a feeling for *words* rather than a capacity for feeling *through* words": that such a style is consequently "incompatible with an interest in sensuous particularity." In Professor Leavis' grouping of poets, Spenser belongs rather with Milton than with Shakespeare and Donne.

This "capacity for feeling through words," this interest in "sensuous particularity" may be seen, for instance, in the following lines from *Hamlet:*

>   Why should the poore be flatterd?
> No, let the candied tongue licke absurd pompe,
> And crooke the pregnant hindges of the knee
> Where thrift may follow fauning.   3. 2. 59–62.
>
> Observe my Vncle, if his occulted guilt
> Doe not it selfe vnkennill in one speech,
> It is a damned ghost that we have seene.   3. 2. 80–82.

Here one observes a subtle merging of thought and sensibility in poetry that is different in kind from the characteristic expression of Spenser and Milton.

A study of Spenser's figures helps to explain this difference, for it has been noted that in his poetry the rhetorical schemes play a far

---

* From Herbert David Rix, *Rhetoric in Spenser's Poetry*. Pennsylvania State College Studies No. 7, State College, Pa, 1940, pp. 76–78 passim. Reprinted by permission of the publisher and the author.

greater part than the tropes, and it is primarily in such tropes as metaphor and metonomy that this merging of thought and sensibility takes place. And in his tropes he seldom aims at the effect achieved by Shakespeare in such expression as "licke absurd pompe" and "it selfe vnkennill in one speech." Spenser's metaphors for the most part are not especially striking; those that do attract one's attention, as for instance,

> In wine and meats she flowd aboue the bancke   *FQ:* 2. 2. 36.
>
> And blow the bellowes to his swelling vanity   *FQ:* 2. 3. 9.

are remarkable not so much for sensuous particularity as for their pictorial—almost picturesque—quality. And this characteristic becomes even more pronounced in Spenser's handling of the extended metaphor—*allegoria*. In short, the main bent of his genius was toward using words, not for the sake of affecting one's sensibilities in the manner of Shakespeare, but in creating out of them patterns of formal beauty, or pictures to entrance the eye. And of course even more important than this is the effect of Spenser's words on the ear, . . . /77/

. . . two words, "mellifluous" and "incantatory," describe exactly the textural qualities of Spenser's verse. . . . /78/

Granting that the figures may be abused, that is, used recklessly for the sole purpose of decoration, we may nevertheless claim for them a place of merit in the creation of great poetry. To Spenser they provided indispensable aid in matters of arrangement and structure, characterization and description, amplification and mood, accomodation of style to subject, and the musical qualities of which he is a supreme master. The observation of Professor Renwick that their rhetorical practice gave the Elizabethan poets a "greater control over language than their elders and greater facility and copiousness than their modern descendants" is by no means an overstatment. For in truth rhetoric must be accounted one of the forces that helped raise English poetry from the depths to which it had fallen after the death of Chaucer to the magnificent summit it attained in the age of Elizabeth.

Hallett Smith

The Use of Conventions in Spenser's Minor Poems, *1961**

When I happened to mention, at a lunch table at the Huntington Library, that I was working on Spenser's minor poems, a young scholar across from me, who is interested in Elizabethan poetry and who has published articles on Spenser, made the remark that the trouble with Spenser's minor poems is that they are so *dull*. Up to that point it hadn't occurred to me to consider whether they were dull or not—as poems; I was studying them to see what material they offered for an investigation that interests me very much—the investigation of what major poetic conventions the Elizabethans used, what meaning these conventions had for the poets and their readers, and what modes of expression arose from the shared understanding of these conventions and meanings. Such study I had found rewarding in a book published eight years ago, and I wished to extend it.

Now a poem may be dull for any one of a number of reasons; if it is dull because of a lack of talent in the poet, certainly nothing can be done about it. A minor poet once complained to Oscar Wilde about the failure of his poems to attract any attention. "It's a conspiracy of silence, Oscar," he said, "what shall I do?" "Join it," said Wilde, "join it." If, however, a poem seems dull to us because the conventions upon which it is based have lost meaning for us, or acquired other meanings, then the kind of investigation I propose may have some value in restoring these old works, removing some of the dark varnish that has obscured their colors and allowing us to see them afresh.

The most familiar example will illustrate what I mean. Dr. Johnson's notorious critique of *Lycidas* may, as a whole, be inexplicable. How

---

* From William Nelson (ed.), *Form and Convention in the Poetry of Edmund Spenser*. New York and London: Columbia University Press, 1961, pp. 122–145. Reprinted by permission of the publisher and the author.

are we to account for a taste which finds in *Lycidas* "the diction . . . harsh, the rhymes uncertain, and the numbers unpleasing"? But we can, I think account for the later part of Johnson's criticism as a failure to see the relevant meaning in a convention. "In this poem there is no nature, for there is no truth; there is no art, for there is nothing new. Its form is that of a pastoral: easy, vulgar, and therefore disgusting; whatever images it can supply are long ago exhausted; and its inherent improbability always forces dissatisfaction on the mind." This view is of course a famous oddity, a warning to critics of their fallibility. Johnson actually thought that no man could have fancied that he read *Lycidas* with pleasure, had he not known the author. Yet John Crowe Ransom in our own time has called it "A Poem Nearly Anonymous." The convention of the pastoral elegy has been understood and validated, most significantly in an essay by George Norlin first published in 1911. No one need have now the difficulty with *Lycidas* which Dr. Johnson had.

I should also perhaps remark that the kind of study I have in mind is to be sharply distinguished from source study. Much laborious work has been done on Spenser's sources; the notes to the Variorum edition attest to this. But the study of a poet's use of conventions is in a way almost opposite to source study, since /124/ when a poet is writing in a convention he is aware of more than one example of the convention he is using. He feels the meaning of that convention and is therefore more significantly guided by it than he is by the wording of any particular example of it. Again, *Lycidas* is a rather obvious instance.

In my book on Elizabethan poetry I discussed *The Shepheardes Calender* and *Colin Clouts Come Home Againe* as part of my treatment of the pastoral eclogue. I tried to establish the thesis that for the Elizabethans pastoral was not, as most modern critics had assumed, an escape from life but a criticism of life and an assertion of the values of *otium* against the values associated with the aspiring mind. In the pastoral eclogue Spenser had a highly conventional form appropriate for his first ambitious attempt to create a new English poetry and equally appropriate for the critical survey of the court and his culture in the time of the poet's maturity. I reached the conclusion that *The Shepheardes Calender* is a very considerable work of art, demonstrating brilliantly that English verse is capable of the most varied and complex effects, all within a traditional mode which had a general European acceptance. I do not know how many readers followed me and agree with that conclusion, but I shall not attempt to defend it further, and I shall leave *The Shepheardes Calender* out of consideration here. I also treated the *Amoretti* and made an attempt to characterize Spenser's sonnets more precisely by showing how they differ in intention, technique, and effect from other sonnet cycles within the convention, such as those of Sidney, Shakespeare, Daniel, and Drayton. I am happy not to have to deal further with the *Amoretti* here, but to leave that subject in the capable hands of Professor Martz. /125/

I propose to focus my attention on four poems: *Muiopotmos, Daphnaida, Epithalamion,* and *Prothalamion.* In approaching these poems I will assume my conclusions based upon *The Shepheardes Calender* and the *Amoretti*—that Spenser was a conscious artist, well aware of the conventions and interested in using them in English to demonstrate the marvelous possibilities of that language, but fundamentally independent and experimental. Whether he succeeds or fails artistically, Spenser seems always insistent upon handling a convention in such a way as to leave upon it the unmistakable stamp of his own mind and style.

I do not take the old-fashioned view that conventions are forced upon the poet and hamper him, so that the critic must be constantly apologetic about the conventions and urge the reader to put up with them for the sake of an occasional break-through into originality. Instead I suppose that the conventions are the primary materials with which the poet works as an artist; this material is neither attractive nor unattractive in itself—everything depends upon what is done with it. I do feel rather old-fashioned, however, when I read Derek Traversi's discussion of Spenser in the Penguin *Guide to English Literature.* He maintains that Spenser exhibits a certain amount of virtuosity, finish, and style, but that on the whole he is a failure because he uses decayed conventions and does not use them very well. Spenser's adaption of the pastoral convention in *The Shepheardes Calender,* for instance, "implies an effort, more or less imposed by circumstances, to evade a direct approach to delicate realities." Mr. Traversi suggests that "already there is a perilous lack of root in this convention (the pastoral). Those whose way of life /126/ has become remote from the real soil cannot be expected to preserve for long the veneer of the soil; and that, translated into social terms, is the meaning of *The Shepheardes Calender.*" The allegorical convention, he goes on to say, was rotten by the time Spenser chose it for *The Faerie Queene.* "To compare Spenser's poem, strictly as an allegorical construction, with *Piers Plowman,* is to be aware of the decay of a convention that had once been valid and had corresponded to a coherent organization of experience."

I am not going to impose my judgment on conventions, as Dr. Johnson imposed his on the pastoral elegy. Nor am I going to plot the life-cycle of a convention and refer to its infancy, adolescence, maturity, senility, and demise. I am merely going to enquire into Spenser's handling of conventions in four poems and see what help this gives me in evaluating him as an artist....

Spenser's *Epithalamion* ... is a poem which needs no defense. It is universally admired, and many readers would agree with DeSelincourt that it is the height of Spenser's poetic achievement. It is also, let us mark, at once the most strictly conventional of all the poems of Spenser and the most personal.

Before we consider the conventional elements in *Epithalamion* and Spenser's method of handling them, it is necessary to return to one of the eclogues in *The Shepheardes Calender* which is in some ways a preliminary exercise for it, as the Dido elegy was for the *Daphnaida*. I mean of course the April eclogue, with its pastoral blazon of Eliza, Queen of Shepherds all. Spenser had already met the problem of form, both structure and versification, /137/ in the lyric in praise of Eliza. Furthermore, he had felt his way toward a solution of the difficult artistic problem of the mingling of tones. The lyric is a "silver song," but it must be kept also within the rustic context of pastoral:

> Ye shepheards daughters, that dwell on the greene,
>   hye you there apace:
> Let none come there, but that Virgins bene,
>   to adorne her grace.
> And when you come, whereas shee is in place,
> See, that your rudenesse doe not you disgrace:
>   Binde your fillets faste,
>   And gird in your waste,
> For more finesse, with a tawdrie lace.   (ll. 127-135)

Other preliminary sketches for the *Epithalamion* appear in Book I of *The Faerie Queene*. One of them comes in a rather surprising place, the episode of the tempting of Redcrosse by the false Una:

> And she herselfe of beautie soueraigne Queene
> Faire Venus seemde vnto his bed to bring
> Her whom he waking euermore did weene
> To be the chastest flowre, that ay did spring
> On earthly braunch, the daughter of a king,
> Now a loose Leman to vile seruice bound:
> And eke the Graces seemed all to sing,
> Hymen io Hymen, dauncing all around,
> While freshest Flora her with Yuie girlond crownd.
>   (I.i.48) /138/

Another, more obvious and appropriate, is the passage describing the marriage of Una and the Redcrosse Knight at the end of Book I. Some of the sonnets in *Amoretti* seem to exhibit motifs which Spenser was to use in the *Epithalamion*, particularly Sonnet 15, a blazon which begins "Ye tradefull merchants that with weary toile," and Sonnet 70, and aubade beginning "Fresh spring, the herald of loues mighty king."

Fortunately we have a recent and excellent study of Spenser's use of conventions in the *Epithalamion*, Thomas M. Greene's essay published in 1957. In Mr. Greene's view, a convention may be regarded as a set of allusions. "A convention exists when the full literary meaning of a word or a line requires a knowledge of many past works in order to be wholly understood.... It follows that the first example one encounters in a convention cannot be read as the poet expected his work to be read." The convention of the epithalamion stretches back to Sappho, but its most influential monuments are three poems by Catullus, especially his No. 61. The form was practised by neo-Latin poets of various nationalities, and by French poets of the Pléiade. The only significant examples before Spenser are Sidney's song of the shepherd Dicus at the marriage of Thyrsis and Kala in the *Arcadia* and Bartholomew Young's poem in his translation of Gil Porto's continuation of Montemayor's *Diana*. But there are many after Spenser, by such poets as Chapman, Ben Jonson, Donne, and Herrick, to mention only the most prominent.

In two respects the first English composers of the epithalamion, Sidney, Young, and Spenser, tend to depart from the classical tradition. First, the epithalamion was traditionally an aristocratic poem, celebrating the nuptials of some noble pair; the poet ac- /139/ cordingly made his encomia as grossly flattering as poems to the eminent usually were. Sidney's and Young's poems are both pastoral, and Spenser's is bourgeois. Second, the English epithalamion tended to favor a refrain or chorus line, which the classical epithalamion did not do except in the hymn to Hymen. As we have already seen in the *Daphnaida*, Spenser favored a refrain line anyway, so we do not have to attribute the repeated "That all the woods may answer and their echo ring" to the influence of his English predecessors.

One can see in his earlier practice also, particularly in the November and April eclogues of *The Shepheardes Calender*, how natural it was for Spenser to develop an elaborate and highly musical stanza for his verse form. He took some hints from the Italian *canzone* for the *Epithalamion* stanza, but he is far more inventive and experimental than he is imitative in his verse form.

Mr. Greene points out that Spenser departed from convention in two ways other than the social class of the participants and the versification. He fused the figures of the poet and the bridegroom when he wrote an epithalamion for his own wedding. This had consequences with respect to what he could do at the climax and at the end. Furthermore, he introduced some humor, which was made possible by the change of social milieu.

It seems to me that Spenser, while respecting and following the traditions of the classical epithalamion, and expecting of course that learned readers would recognize the allusions and applaud his graceful mastery of them, also took pains to make the poem as native, immediate, and personal as he could, within the limits of decorum. In the first stanza, a traditional invocation of /140/ the Muses, he reminds the reader that he is the poet of the *Tears of the Muses* in the volume called *Complaints*. In the fourth stanza he reminds the reader that he lives in Ireland and has a personal pride in the details of his own geographical environment:

> Ye nymphs of Mulla which with carefull heed
> The siluer scaly trouts doe tend full well,
> And greedy pikes which vse therein to feed
> (Those trouts and pikes all others doo excell)
> And ye likewise which keepe the rushy lake,
> Where none doo fishes take . . .   (ll. 56–61)

It is a realistic picture, presented insistently in the foreground against a perspective of Roman deities, traditional symbolic figures, and the whole evocative tradition of the wedding song. The merchant's daughters, the young men of the town who ring the bells, the boys who run up and down the street—they all seem like figures from actual contemporary life. Yet the boys shout, as if they were the creatures of Catullus, "Hymen io Hymen."

The imagery of the description of the bride is emblematic, as it is so often in the *Amoretti*; Spenser is here strongly influenced by the Song of Songs, which he must have considered an epithalamion;

> Her lips lyke cherryes charming men to byte,
> Her brest like to a bowle of cream vncrudded,
> Her paps lyke lyllies budded,
> Her snowie necke lyke to a marble towre,
> And all her body like a pallace fayre, /141/
> Ascending vppe with many a stately stayre,
> To honors seat and chastities sweet bowre.
>   (ll. 174–180)

Yet in contrast to this highly stylized poetry we have the semi-comic catalogue of night noises:

> Let not the shriech Oule, nor the Storke be heard:
> Nor the night Rauen that still deadly yels,
> Nor damned ghosts cald vp with mighty spels,
> Nor griesly vultures make vs once affeard:
> Ne let the unpleasant Quyre of Frogs still croking
> Make vs to wish theyr choking.
> Let none of these theyr drery accents sing;
> Ne let the woods them answer, nor theyr eccho ring.
> (ll. 345–352)

I think Mr. Greene is right in seeing more structure in the poem than the commentators usually do. If the first stanza, the invocation, is considered prefatory, the rest of the poem consists of two 10-stanza sections on each side of the two central stanzas about the church ceremony itself. Then each of the 10-stanza sections is divided into units of 3-4-3. This is an architectural scheme, not found in the conventional epithalamion, but very characteristic of Spenser (recall the seven sevens of seven in *Daphnaida*). He finally addresses his poem:

> Be unto her a goodly ornament
> And for short time an endlesse moniment.

Such design, he felt, was suitable for a poem which was to be ornament and monument. If this strictness of design seem too /142/ stiff or too pedantic for modern readers, perhaps the dazzling and varied musical qualities of the poem will provide compensation. The music is possible because the convention Spenser was following took care of many problems and left him free for song.

Prothalamion is even more completely lyric than the *Epithalamion*. It is a spousal or betrothal song for the two daughters of the Earl of Worcester; its date in the autumn of 1596 may thus be established with some exactness. The name *Prothalamion* seems to be a coinage of Spenser's. No other Elizabethan uses it except Drayton, who was clearly influenced by Spenser. There was, however, a convention of such poems. Dan Norton, who has traced the tradition most fully, shows that betrothal ceremonies, in life and in fiction, encouraged the composition of poems, but that the authors of them derived their motifs largely from the convention of the epithalamion.

Spenser, however, makes use of another tradition—one in which he himself had already experimented. It is the tradition of river poems.

Sixteen years before the *Prothalamion* Spenser had composed, in Latin, a poem called *Epithalamion Thamensis*. It was never published and is now unknown, but one can guess what it was like from other examples of the genre. Later on, Spenser composed an elaborate account of the marriage of the Thames and the Medway for the eleventh canto of Book IV of *The Faerie Queene*. And in the very personal and topical poem *Colin Clouts Come Home Againe* (1591) he inserted a passage of 55 lines describing the marriage of two Irish rivers. As worked out by Osgood forty years ago,[20] the principal themes or motifs of river poems, as practised by Camden, Leland, Vallans, and /143/ Spenser, were three: (1) a journey of some swans, (2) a marriage of two rivers, and (3) some topographic, antiquarian review of places on the banks of the two rivers.

The obvious qualities of such a poem are learning, especially of an antiquarian sort, facility at mythical invention or adaptation, and copiousness of description. It is the kind of thing for which the talents of Michael Drayton later turned out to be appropriate.

Spenser, in writing the *Prothalamion,* modified the convention in two ways: he returned, as he was so prone to do, to Chaucer and introduced some elements of the dream vision and complaint. The poet opens with a description of the calm, pleasant day, which contrasts with his own mood of "sullein care, / Through discontent of my long fruitlesse stay / In prince's court, and expectation vayne / Of idle hopes, which still do fly away." He sees the water-nymphs gathering flowers; two beautiful swans appear, and the nymphs strew flowers before them and one of them sings a congratulatory lay. Then he reverts to his personal associations by mentioning London as his birthplace, his "most kindly nurse," and recalling that at Essex House, formerly the palace of his patron Leicester, "Oft I gayned giftes and goodly grace / Of that great lord, which therein wont to dwell, / Whose want too well now feedes my freendles case."

The other modification is to extend the allusiveness of the poem not into antiquarian or topographical lore, but to lively current matters of interest. There are puns on the names of Somerset and Devereux. The studious lawyers who now inhabit the Temple are mentioned as well as the ancient Knights Templar. A whole stanza is devoted to the Earl of Essex, /144/

> Great Englands glory and the Worlds wide wonder,
> Whose dreadfull name, late through all Spaine did thunder,
> And Hercules two pillors standing neere,
> Did make to quake and feare.   (ll. 145–149)

Epithalamion

The rather cold conventional elements of the river song have been relieved by the reflective, somewhat melancholy tone of the poet—a tone which contrasts with the happiness of the occasion. As he says,

> But Ah here fits not well
> Olde woes but ioyes to tell
> Against the bridale daye, which is not long:
>   Sweet *Themmes* runne softly, till I end my Song.

Furthermore, the journalistic allusiveness of the poem balances the artifice of the nymphs and the symbolic swans.

No novelties of structure mark the *Prothalamion*; it is less formal than the *Epithalamion*, and, perhaps for that reason, only half as long. The movement of the stanzas has been much admired, and the versification in general, as well as Spenser's deftness in manipulating the stanza toward the refrain. That refrain has paid the price of its popularity by serving as ironic contrast in that other poem which uses events on the Thames as reflections of the values of contemporary life. I mean of course *The Waste Land*.

If we try to generalize about Spenser's use of conventions in the minor poems I think we must make at least the following observations. Spenser was a poet to whom the conventions were still alive. He saw them used by contemporary French and Italian /145/ writers as well as by the ancients. In fact, I do not think that he felt there was as much chronological difference between the ancients and the moderns as do we. In some sense Eliot's famous remark can be applied to Spenser, that for him the whole of European literature from Homer to the present day had a contemporaneous existence.

To be sure, Spenser adapted the conventions to his own use. In doing this he was following in the footsteps of his master Chaucer and showing the way to his disciple Milton. Like them he felt that the personal element in poetry, the reflection of the mind and temper of the individual writer, is expressed most vividly when it is embedded in a convention. Like them also, he saw to it that his work was distinctively English, that it displayed an instinctive and intimate love of English rivers and flowers and trees, and an artist's pride in the English language.

Versification

Robert Beum

Some Observations on Spenser's Verse Forms, 1963*

I

In English alone there are more studies of Spenser's prosody than one can profitably read. No one has ever neglected an opportunity to make at least a passing comment on the verse of the *Faerie Queene,* and perhaps only the versification of *Paradise Lost* has been studied more intently than that of the *Shepheardes Calender.* Few of our poets have gotten such a nearly equal division of labor between message and metric. And yet some teasing problems remain. Most of the work on the prosody is, in fact, limited to the *Faerie Queene* and the *Shepheardes Calender;* most of that, in turn, has taken the form of special studies of particular aspects of the stanzas, especially of native and continental sources and influences. It is impossible to form a distinct view of the whole range of Spenser's verse from a reading of all this scattered study. And yet that is exactly what is needed. If, after taking a vow of abstinence from all ingenuity, we can relate the form and chronology of Spenser's art in such a way as to see in it a distinct rationale, we shall get, I think, a more complete understanding of the poetry itself. The study of the verse patterns emerging /181/ out of a great poet's work accumulated over a lifetime can be fully as fascinating as the study of symbols and influences. To watch a great intelligence and sensibility come into its own, perhaps after some false starts, through the discovery of a form, or a number of forms, that finally allows it the fullest expression, and to follow the poet's continual shaping of the form to make it ever more flexible—this is the kind of story that, widening our curiosity and admiration, widens our humanity. Some sort of unified and unify-

---

* From *Neuphilologische Mitteilungen,* LXIV, 1963, 180–196. Reprinted by permission of the editors and the author.

ing view of the body of a poet's work is, of course, what commonly emerges from biographical and from scholarly or critical studies. But most of these books and articles are concerned mainly, and often almost exclusively, with genre, or with the emergent pattern of taste and theme. There has been, at least in our own tradition, an unfortunate tendency to forget the fact that idea, feeling, and imagination, however tremendous and however fraught with interesting and half-traceable influences, yield up their meaning and take hold of us only through particular words and lines and stanzas arranged in particular ways— through particular phonemes and their intervals, if you will. In Spenser's case there are more pressing reasons which warrant such a study of formal development. After four centuries, the achievement of the Spenserian stanza is still dubious, and in fact the elaborateness of nearly all the verse of Spenser's later years calls his judgment and even his integrity into question. Now there is no quarreling with one's taste in stanzas, but at least we should be able to determine whether Spenser devised intricate stanzas to suit his vision, or whether he conjured visions merely to indulge his technical virtuosity and to ingratiate himself with his queen.

At the same time, I am not interested primarily in adding to the literature of Spenser's defense. I have simply wanted to find the rationale of his choice of verse forms over a period of about thirty years. One wants to know why he worked in certain forms in certain years, and why so much of his later poetry is elaborate in form, and how he meets certain exigencies arising from the decision to work in such difficult forms. /182/

II

To view the whole of Spenser's poetry, looking at the verse forms in terms of the publication dates and probable dates of composition, is to see that the work reveals three distinct periods.

First, in the early 1570's, is the apprenticeship: a few years of modest imitation and of translation which culminate in the vigorous and eclectic experimentation of the *Shepheardes Calender*. In the manner of the young virtuoso who ends his apprentice years and begins his real career with a bravura showpiece, Spenser flourishes in his pastoral a dozen (a baker's dozen) forms. He manages them with technical mastery but without realizing their limitations for future work. It is perhaps an innate (and not merely youthful) idealism, as much as it is this youthful exuberance and facility, which accounts for the variety and ambition of these forms: a less idealistic temperament would have been more satisfied with tried forms, and less hopeful that such novel and elaborate measures would prove serviceable later on. The forms that would have been most familiar to any sixteenth century English poet are the very ones not found in the *Shepheardes Calender:* rime royal, ottava rima, blank verse, and pentameter couplet are missing, and the ballad stanza is used only once.

The period of maturity, which begins conveniently around 1580, is wholly dominated, till the last few years, by stanzas of seven, eight, and nine lines. It is a time of rime royals, of ottava rimas,[1] and of the *Faerie Queene* stanza, forms which have much in common (each is a roomy stanza and each follows a pattern of alternating rhyme which leads at last to a couplet). As a /183/ matter of fact, not a single one of the minor poems of the decade 1580–90 is cast in anything other than an alternately rhyming septain or octave. Even *Colin Clouts Come Home Again* is written in a series of linked sections of irregularly alternating rhymes, and the sections themselves are of seven or of eight lines.

The first period is not at all puzzling. Spenser's way is the way of many an English poet: first the young poet, in a mood of high emulation, gives various traditional or current forms a try, and then even launches out into novelties. Of course, the precise relationships between the various prosodies of the months in the *Shepheardes Calender* have not been fully explored. The particular measures quite possibly bear subtler relationships to the subjects and moods of the particular months, and to one another, than criticism has as yet enabled us to see. But, for present purposes, it is enough to note that the very virtuosity is perfectly natural, and marks out a period for us, or, strictly speaking, terminates a period. But Spenser's restricting himself, throughout most of his maturity, to a very few forms similar enough to make relatively easy a movement back and forth from one to another, arouses one's curiosity as to why he adopted these rather than certain others.

The question becomes all the more interesting when one sees that in the whole of the *Shepheardes Calender* and in the juvenilia which precedes it there is not a single rime royal to predict the abundant royals of Spenser's maturity. The switch to this septain, and the parallel and complementary evolution of the *Faerie Queene* stanza, is attended by another strong change: Spenser "kicks the geese out of the boat." He tends to be an alliterative poet, but the alliteration in his later poetry is mild indeed compared with that of the *Shepheardes Calender*.

---

[1] *Muipotmos* was almost certainly composed at some time between 1589 and 1591. *Virgils Gnat*, the other ottava rima poem, is of uncertain date; it is usually assigned to the years 1576–80. The verse form itself may help argue for a date closer to 1580 than to 1576.

These two decisions, the one aginst a markedly alliterative verse, and the other in favor of a stanza not even to be found in the early poem, are in themselves evidence enough that the pastoral is to be regarded as the last poem of Spenser's youth, rather /184/ than the first one of his maturity. He found himself, as poets nearing maturity commonly do, in need of a form or two which would be available for rather various themes and tones, and which would be at the same time suitable to his own particular inclinations. Poets begin to favor a form or a few forms which they can learn, or have already learned, so thoroughly that they can, as Yeats says, sing them while they are "half-asleep or riding upon a journey." Spenser's choice is a natural one: stanzas of seven, eight, and nine lines provide space for working up the increasing complexity and richness of maturing vision; they are right for youthful lyricism as it turns more and more meditative, and they are right for the narrative poem too, in that a single stanza of such length allows the poet to take a full step forward. Spenser found his idiom in these stanzas, just as Browning found, at last, one of his great strengths in dramatic blank verse, and Yeats one of his in the recurring octaves of his later years. One sees too that forms which allow alternating rhyme are peculiarly suited to Spenser: the richer, more intricate, music answers to something in his very soul. And his is an expansive, not an epigrammatic, temperament; it is easy to see why the pentameter couplet had so little attraction for him. The rime royal in particular is a splendidly logical choice: from the time of Chaucer it had remained easily the most popular of long stanzas, and Spenser's obvious love of Chaucer and Marot would have gotten him into the habit of thinking in it.

But why, then, are there no rime royals in the *Shepheardes Calender?* I have already suggested that Spenser's avoidance of the form may be atrributed in part to the youthful impulse to essay new and ingenious forms, a trait which fits both Spenser's ambition and idealism, and his genetic facility with versification. The Renaissance poet, like Renaissance men generally, was curiously equipoised: he was happy, and even obliged, to follow tradition; and yet he could not resist the bold exploration and self-assertion of the times. If he followed convention in /185/ genre and in the decorum of the genre, he was as likely to follow his own bent in his choice or handling of metric. The subject matter and the moods of Spenser's pastoral are pretty conventional; the calendrical scheme, and the prosody (in its variety, its particularities, and its impingement upon syntax) constitute a distinct individuality. In *Lycidas* there are some striking departures from the convention—and Milton is far too deferent to the tradition not to acknowledge them as such.

The choice of verse forms in this middle period, then, shows a distinct logic. Spenser settles upon a few viable patterns. Experimentation is pretty much limited to that which is necessary to the perfection of a single form, the *Faerie Queene* stanza. In the *Daphnaïda*, it is true, he introduces a slight variation on regular rime royal, and curiously no one has been able to account for the innovation, though everyone has wondered about it. Nothing about the theme, tone, or structure of the poem calls for anything except an ordinary royal. And yet, with poets who pay as much attention to prosody as Spenser and Milton, one must assume, I think, that such changes are always intentional and functional. In the case of *Daphnaïda*, one answer which possesses frequency and simplicity is that this poem, unlike any of Spenser's other verse of his middle period, is an occasional and commemorative poem. The slight innovation exists, perhaps, as a token of personal involvement, as a mark of speciality. One notices that Spenser devises unique verse for his other commemoratives: for the *Amoretti* and *Epithalamion*, presented to his betrothed, and for the *Prothalamion*, a gift for the Somersets.

These latter poems pose another difficulty. The fact that they are occasional poems does, I believe, go quite some way toward explaining their uniqueness in form. But their unprecedented elaborateness is still another matter and calls for a detailed explanation—which, of course, can mean only careful speculation. The *Faerie Queene* stanza too cannot be /186/ explained in terms of occasion. The appearance of all this elaborate verse late in Spenser's career presents a really engaging problem. It looked as if, after the inevitable passing of youthful exuberance and showmanship, Spenser had settled upon traditional and flexible stanzas of the general length and pattern of rime royal and ottava rima. And then here he is, toward the end of his life, being exotic and experimental again.

In a way, as regards the poems of courtship and marriage, occasion does provide us with a part of the answer. These poems appear late because Spenser happened to marry late, and because the Somerset ladies married not long after the poet himself. As far as I can see, there is no particular connection between the elaborateness of these poems and the fact that they appear at the end of Spenser's career, other than mere occasion. There is, I think, no reason to suppose that they would have been less elaborate, had the occasions been earlier. The key to these poems is rather a matter of personal involvement. One can see a distinct formula working out as regards all of the occasional verse (excepting, for no reason that has occurred to me, *Astrophel*). Spenser devises special forms, as suiting the speciality of the occasions; and the more intimately involved he is, the more unusual or exotic the verse structure.

Thus *Colin Clouts Come Home Again* is a spirited allegory of Spenser's disenchanting experience at court in 1589–90. Its rhyming and its line groupings are boldly irregular. The *Daphnaïda*, a poem Spenser no doubt felt obliged to write for his poet friend Arthur Gorges, is an elegy on a lady Spenser could not have known well, and possibly had not even met.[2] The verse is a simple variation on an otherwise perfectly normal /187/ rime royal. A stanza as intricate as that of the *Epithalamion* or even of the *Prothalamion* would hardly have been appropriate to the matter, nor would it have occurred to Spenser to try to write extended allegorical narrative in *canzone*-like stanzas. Nevertheless, Spenser does give the poem a touch of prosodic distinctiveness.

The *Prothalamion* may well have been commissioned. In any event, Spenser was then living at Essex House, where the two Somerset ladies were married. He was in the midst of things, and no doubt the event stirred memory of his own wedding only two years earlier. Its verse is only less intricate and difficult than that of the *Amoretti* and the *Epithalamion*. These latter poems carry intricacy still forward, and they are, of course, respectively the poet's courtship and marriage poems. A closer look at them is perhaps in order.

The delicate and extraordinary form of the *Amoretti* seems to be a prosodic—that is, an oblique—statement of the poet's love. He is presenting Elizabeth Boyle with a gift of sonnets formally unique (in English, that is; the form is Marot's) and quite difficult; she is to see how hard he has worked and how special she is in his eyes. And he is at the same time accepting the role of the lover who will play the game of courtship according to the elaborate code. The prosody takes its cue, or one of its cues, from the ingenuity of the game: one must be playful and skillful. There is no contradiction, only the delightful Renaissance tension.

The marriage song itself is the most elaborate of Spenser's occasional (or other) poems, and the reason seems to be that it is a gift, and a gift for his own bride rather than for someone more remote. But at the same time that it is Spenser's most personal poem, it is also suprapersonal: it is a vision of ideal marriage and ideal womanhood which quite transcends its "short time." Its elaborateness, then, constitutes a paradox. It is an indirection, an obliquity, which expresses, on the one hand, personal involvement of the deepest sort, and on the /188/ other, the impersonality of ritual, and the transcendent aspect of marriage itself.

---

[2] Arthur Gorges married Douglas Howard in 1584; she died in 1590. Spenser was in Ireland nearly all this time; it is doubtful that his first visit to England was earlier than November of 1589, and once in London he would have divided most of his time between the court and Ponsonby, who had agreed to publish, and quickly did publish, the first instalment of the *Faerie Queene*.

Epithalamion

The prosody is at once warmth and realized distance. In the vibrance of this expansive epodic stanza, as in its euphony, we see Spenser's joy in the day and in the prospect of the future. In its largeness and intricacy we see his wish to present a wedding gift suitably generous and hard-wrought and formal—expensive, as it were. The high elaborateness is, once again, his way of showing his bride how much loving trouble he has gone to, and how delighted he is; at the same time, it is his way of obtaining a formality appropriate to the ritual and to the lofty conception. Poems of this sort are rare in our day, but perhaps not quite extinct. Dylan Thomas's fine "Poem in October," for example, is a lyric that in its elaborately epodic and cross-rhyming syllabic prosody similarly fuses both ecstasy and the formality and dignity of commemoration.

At the same time, occasion and the degree of Spenser's personal involvement are not quite, perhaps, the whole story. Spenser obviously *welcomed* the occasions. They put him under obligation, but they also gave him an opportunity to do something large and something extra. He was by nature too metrically inventive to remain wholly content with the very rime royals and ottavas and similar forms he had adopted as his characteristic verse idiom. These stanzas were, quite literally, too easy for him, and they could not generate that rich liturgy of cross-woven music peculiar to epodic or otherwise intricate stanzas. Generally suitable as the septains and octaves were to Spenser's bent and experience, still they could not provide the fullest fruition of his powers. . . .

John Erskine

From The Elizabethan Lyric, *1905**

The mass of curious erudition in this lyric [the *Epithalamion*] is characteristic of Spenser and his times. The wonder is that the singing quality of the lines is so little retarded by it. To Spenser the muses were indeed "ye learned sisters." He uses astronomy in Chaucer's elaborate fashion to fix the date of the wedding-day. He expounds in one winged stanza half a dozen points of folk-lore. On classical mythology he has ever a ready word: twenty-four deities are mentioned, and their functions described; the poet can even stop to enlarge on an unfamiliar legend of Diana. /191/

This pagan background is made to accord, strangely enough, with the thoroughly Christian elements in the poem. To mingle the two systems was not indeed unusual with Renaissance poets, but Spenser justifies the use by making the pagan deities represent the mystery of nature, and confining the Christian system to the expression of the soul; so that there is no conflict. He realizes this pagan sense of the mysterious personality in nature best in the lovely prayer to the rising moon...

If each motive in the *Epithalamium* be considered by itself, it will appear that Spenser has used entirely conventional material. The effect of the whole, however, is spontaneous. The explanation is that the poet has designed situations out of which the old motives seem naturally to rise. For example, as the poem is the culmination of his sonnets, and as a favorite theme in the sonnet-series is... the physical description of the lady, it is but natural that Spenser should have such a description here. He puts new life into the theme, however, by describing his mistress /192/ at the moment when, after long and impatient waiting, he

---

* From John Erskine, *The Elizabethan Lyric*. New York: Columbia University Press, 1905, pp. 190–192. Reprinted by permission of the publisher and the author.

catches the first sight of her, dressed for her bridal. The extravagant terms of the sonnets, "ivory forehead," "cherry lips," and "eyes like saphyres," here seem not only excusable but natural, because we already understand the poet's love-delirium. The elevation of tone is sustained here also by the added description of the lady's spiritual and mental virtues—the Platonic touch.

Suggestions for Papers

Setting your "modern mentality" as far aside as possible, write a paper in which you try to imagine exactly how Spenser's contemporaries (the more perceptive ones, that is) would have read and responded to the *Epithalamion*.

Demonstrate how a modern reader's understanding and appreciation of the *Epithalamion* is enhanced by a knowledge of the Renaissance milieu.

To what extent can a reader understand and appreciate the *Epithalamion* without a knowledge of the conventions which Spenser is following?

In what ways did Spenser's following certain conventions actually aid him in creating a successful poem?

In what ways does the poem reflect—in both content and style—the tastes, attitudes, and ideas of the age in which he lived?

Discuss Platonic or anti-Platonic (or unPlatonic) values or elements in the poem.

Discuss the *Epithalamion* as a poem informed by the attitudes and conventions of Courtly Love.

Discuss the attitude toward love expressed in the *Epithalamion*.

Discuss the Protestant aspect of the poem.

Despite its great merits, the *Epithalamion* would not seem to be a very modern-minded person's "cup of tea." Why is this the case, and what does the modern-minded reader miss by ignoring this poem?

It may be that certain kinds of subjects and certain attitudes or tones are especially congenial to the inherent nature of poetry, so that, other things being equal, a poem which adopts them will be more satisfying than a poem which does not. Does the *Epithalamion* owe something of its greatness to a special affinity which exists between its matter and manner and the character of poetry itself as an art?

Epithalamion 133

Locate in the criticism that has been written about the poem, major differences of opinon; evaluate them with a view toward reaching a sane and comprehensive understanding of the poem.

Point out defects in the *Epithalamion* and evaluate their importance in relation to the poem as a whole.

Defend the poem against the charge of wordiness.

Justify (or attack) the poem's mixture of Christian and pagan elements.

In what sense is it a mistake to identify the speaker in the poem with Edmund Spenser himself?

Why has this poem been given such high praise for nearly four hundred years?

Analyze Spenser's use of the *rhetorical* devices he learned in school.

Define the three or four distinctive aesthetic features or characteristics of the poem, and then show how Spenser's use of Elizabethan rhetorical devices in part accounts for the existence of these features.

Discuss the poem in terms of Spenser's employment of *inventio, dispositio,* and *elocutio,* the three major rhetorical aspects of a composition which were recognized by Renaissance writers.

Was the "smoothness" of Spenser's style dictated to him by Renaissance fashion and philosophy, by his own temperament, or by both?

What is unusual about the prosody (versification) of the poem?

Write a detailed analysis of the *Epithalamion's* matching of sound and sense. Explore the poem in terms of words and rhythms whose physical qualities are appropriate to their meaning.

Does the *Epithalamion* gain from being read *aloud? How so?*

Examine carefully the way Spenser employs alliteration in this poem.

Write a discussion based upon a careful study of the poem's *rhyme.*

Explain and justify Spenser's use of an extremely elaborate verse form.

In the *Epithalamion,* Spenser does not tell a story, but *envisions* the events of the marriage day and night. The poem may be said to be organized in terms of a visionary chronology. What advantages accrue to Spenser through his adoption of this technique?

Present and evaluate several critical interpretations of the poem's *tornata* (final section).

What gives the poem its *universality*?

Is there any humor in the poem? If so, what is its effect?

In what ways does the *Epithalamion* show *balance*, and what is the significance of this balance?

Explore in detail Spenser's ability (or failure) to fuse harmoniously the various materials and tones of the poem.

Compare some aspect of Spenser's *Epithalamion* with some aspect of the epithalamions written by Sidney, Donne, Ben Jonson, or other contemporaries.

Which is the more impressive poem, the *Epithalamion* or the *Prothalamion*? Why?

Discuss ways in which the writing of his *Epithalamion* may have given Spenser ideas for the *Prothalamion*.

A poet is most likely to do his best work when he is writing about a subject he knows and likes well, and when his forms and techniques are those in which he has previously had practice. Discuss the poem in the light of this truism.

How is the figure of Cinthia in the twenty-first stanza to be interpreted? As Queen Elizabeth I? As the pagan goddess? As both?

Spenser idealizes the river, the local merchants, and other aspects of the Irish town where the marriage took place. Is this idealization really justifiable or is it a mere glamourizing or sentimentalizing distortion of actualities?

In what ways does the success of the poem depend upon Spenser's *indirection* (that is, upon implication rather than explicit statement)?

Additional Readings

NOTE: Cortlandt Van Winkle's edition of the *Epithalamion* (1926) is the most helpful one available in English. Its Introduction, Notes, and Bibliography are comprehensive and extremely accurate; the serious student of the poem should consult this edition at once. Volume 2 of the famous Variorum edition of Spenser's *Works* (1947), edited by Edwin Greenlaw and others, offers a text of the poem together with extensive notes and critical and scholarly commentary culled from many sources. Another absolutely indispensable book is Case's *English Epithalamies* (1896), which collects most of the epithalamiums written in English between 1581 and 1731 and offers a detailed history of the genre. For a sound and well-written introduction to Spenser's poetry as a whole, the reader should consult W. L. Renwick's *Edmund Spenser, an Essay on Renaissance Poetry* (1925).

Editions

Greenlaw, Edwin, and others, eds. *The Works of Edmund Spenser: A Variorum Edition: Volume Two, The Minor Poems.* Baltimore: Johns Hopkins Press, 1947.

Renwick, W. L., ed. *Daphnäida and Other Poems.* London: The Scholartis Press, 1929.

Van Winkle, Cortlandt, ed. *Epithalamion.* New York: F. S. Crofts & Co., 1926.

Reference, Bibliography

Atkinson, Dorothy F. *Edmund Spenser: A Bibliographical Supplement.* Baltimore: Johns Hopkins Press, 1937.

Carpenter, F. I. *A Reference Guide to Edmund Spenser.* Gloucester, Mass.: Peter Smith, 1950.

McNeir, Waldo F., and Foster Provost, *Annotated Bibliography of Edmund Spenser, 1937–1960.* Duquesne Studies: Philological Series, Volume Three. Duquesne University Press, 1962.

Osgood, Charles G. *A Concordance to the Poems of Edmund Spenser.* Washington, D. C.: Carnegie Institution of Washington, 1915.

Stephens, Robert F. *A Check List of Masters' Theses on Edmund Spenser.* Charlottesville: Bibliographical Society of the University of Virginia, c/o University of Virginia Library, 1950.

Whitman, C. H. *A Subject-Index to the Poems of Edmund Spenser.* New Haven: Yale University Press, 1918.

Spenser: General Criticism

Nelson, William. *The Poetry of Edmund Spenser.* New York: Columbia University Press, 1963.

Osgood, Charles G. *Poetry as a Means of Grace.* Princeton: Princeton University Press; London: H. Milford, Oxford University Press, 1941.

Yeats, William Butler. "Edmund Spenser," *Essays and Introductions.* New York: The Macmillan Co., 1961.

Epithalamion: Origins, Genre

Hamer, Douglas. "Spenser's Marriage." *Review of English Studies,* VII (1931), 271–290.

McPeek, James A. S. "The Major Sources of Spenser's Epithalamion." *Journal of English and Germanic Philology,* 35 (1936), 183–213.

Norton, Dan. "The Tradition of Prothalamia," in *English Studies in Honor of James Southall Wilson.* Charlottesville: The University of Virginia Press, 1951, pp. 223–241.

Smith, Hallett. *Elizabethan Poetry: A Study in Conventions, Meaning and Expression.* Cambridge, Mass.: Harvard University Press, 1952.

Epithalamion: Philosophy

Ellrodt, Robert. *Neoplatonism in the Poetry of Spenser.* Librairie E. Droz, 1960.

Kristeller, Paul Oskar. "Renaissance Platonism," in *Renaissance Thought: The Classic, Scholastic, and Humanist Strains.* New York: Harper & Row, 1961.

Nelan, Thomas P. *Catholic Doctrines in Spenser's Poetry.* Unpublished thesis, New York University, 1943.

Padelford, F. M. "Spenser and the Theology of Calvin," *Modern Philology,* XII (1914), 1–18.

Wind, Edgar. *Pagan Mysteries in the Renaissance.* New Haven: Yale University Press, 1958.

Epithalamion: Imagery and Symbolism

Glazier, Lyle. "The Nature of Spenser's Imagery," *Modern Language Quarterly*, XVI (1955), 300–310.

Hieatt, A. Kent. *Short Time's Endless Monument: The Symbolism of the Numbers in Edmund Spenser's Epithalamion.* New York: Columbia University Press, 1960.

Hopper, Vincent. *Medieval Number Symbolism.* New York: Columbia University Press, 1938.

Lotspeich, H. G. *Classical Mythology in Spenser's Poetry.* Princeton: Princeton University Press, 1932.

Epithalamion: Language, Style

Baldwin, C. S. *Renaissance Literary Theory and Practice.* New York: Columbia University Press, 1939.

Clark, D. L. *Rhetoric and Poetry in the Renaissance.* New York: Columbia University Press, 1922.

Rubel, Veré. *Poetic Diction in the English Renaissance from Skelton Through Spenser.* London: Oxford University Press, 1941.

Epithalamion: Versification

Davis, B. E. C. *Edmund Spenser: A Critical Study.* Cambridge: Cambridge University Press, 1933.

Appendices

I

Edmund Gosse, in his anthology *English Odes* (1881, Introduction, p. 12), offered the following definition of the *ode*: "any strain of enthusiastic and exalted lyrical verse, directed to a fixed purpose and dealing progressively with one dignified theme." C. F. Johnson, in his *Forms of English Poetry* (1904, pp. 147–8), produced an excellent commentary on Gosse's definition.

II

Catullus's epithalamium LXI, stanzas 1–2, trans. Robert Beum:

> Collis o Heliconii
> cultor, Uraniae genus,
> qui rapis teneram ad virum
> virginem, o Hymenaee Hymen,
>   o Hymen Hymenaee,
>
> cinge tempora floribus
> suave olentis amaraci,
> flammeum cape, laetus huc
> huc veni niveo gerens
>   luteum pede soccum . . .
>
> We call to Urania's child,
> Helicon's young wanderer
> Hymen—Hymen, who brings
> That fortune, who brings the joy
> Of the tender girl
> To the joy of the man!
>
> With marjoram (sweetness to spare!)
> Make your hair a flourish,
> Mask, set off those god-white feet
> With flaming sandals, and glide
> To this place, O soon
> And all joy, to this place . . .